THE DESERT GARDEN

You Can Be Water-Wise and Still Create a Lush,
Colorful, Native Oasis

DIAN EATON

PAINTED SUNSET PUBLISHING

© Copyright 2024–Dian Eaton All Rights Reserved

Published 2024 Painted Sunset Publishing

The content contained within this book may not be reproduced, duplicated or transmitted without direct written permission from the author or the publisher.

Under no circumstances will any blame or legal responsibility be held against the publisher, or author, for any damages, reparation, or monetary loss due to the information contained within this book, either directly or indirectly.

Legal Notice:

This book is copyright-protected. It is only for personal use. You cannot amend, distribute, sell, use, quote or paraphrase any part or the content within this book, without the consent of the author or publisher.

Disclaimer Notice:

Please note the information contained within this document is for educational and entertainment purposes only. All effort has been executed to present accurate, up-to-date, reliable, complete information. No warranties of any kind are declared or implied. Readers acknowledge that the author is not engaged in the rendering of legal, financial, medical or professional advice. The content within this book has been derived from various sources. Please consult a licensed professional before attempting any techniques outlined in this book.

By reading this document, the reader agrees that under no circumstances is the author responsible for any losses, direct or indirect, that are incurred as a result of the use of the information contained within this document, including, but not limited to, errors, omissions, or inaccuracies.

Books by Dian Eaton

The Garden series:

THE MEADOW GARDEN

THE POLLINATOR GARDEN

THE DESERT GARDEN

Children's Books:

SCOOTER – The Little Tiger with a Big Heart

HENRY HUMMINGBIRD – and the Great Bird Song Concert

Regional History and Humor:

IS IT TRUE WHAT THEY SAY ABOUT DIXIE?

HOW TO TALK LIKE A SOUTHERNER

*For my daughter, Kimberly, and my grandchildren, Ryan and Kyra.
You are my heart.*

Contents

Introduction	11
1. FOUNDATIONS OF DESERT GARDENING	15
1.1 Defining Dry Climate and Its Impact on Gardening	16
1.2 The Science of Drought Tolerance in Plants	17
1.3 Topography and Microclimates: What You Need to Know	20
1.4 Soil Types and Their Roles in Dry Climate Gardens	22
1.5 The Importance of Native Plants in Eco-Gardening	24
1.6 Addressing Common Misconceptions About Dry Climate Gardening	26
2. DESIGNING YOUR DESERT GARDEN	31
2.1 Principles of Xeriscape Design: More Than Just Cacti	32
2.2 Creating Color and Contrast with Drought-Tolerant Plants	34
2.3 To Turf or Not to Turf	38
2.4 Innovative Uses of Rocks and Gravel in Design	45
2.5 Shade Planning: Maximizing Comfort and Plant Health	49
2.6 Paths and Walkways: Functional and Water-Smart Solutions	50
2.7 Mulching Techniques Specific to Dry Climates	52
2.8 The Desert Meadow Garden	54
3. PLANT SELECTION AND CARE	61
3.1 Cacti and Succulents: Choosing the Right Plants for Your Garden	62
3.2 Deep Dive into Desert Perennials: Long-Lived Beauty	71
3.3 The Perennial Desert Rose	75
3.4 Annuals and Biennials That Thrive in Arid Zones	81

3.5 Trees and Shrubs for Dry Conditions: A Detailed Guide	84
3.6 Iconic Palm Trees	87
3.7 The Role of Grasses in a Dry Garden	93
3.8 Care and Maintenance of Drought-Resistant Plants	94
4. ATTRACTING WILDLIFE AND SUPPORTING BIODIVERSITY	97
4.1 Designing Pollinator-Friendly Gardens in Dry Climates	97
4.2 Best Plants for Attracting Beneficial Insects	100
4.3 Water Features for Wildlife in Arid Gardens	102
4.4 Shelter and Nesting: Supporting Fauna Diversity	104
4.5 Seasonal Considerations for Wildlife Support	105
4.6 *SPECIAL SECTION!* Desert Wildlife Guests	107
5. WATER MANAGEMENT STRATEGIES	113
5.1 Drip Irrigation Systems: Setup and Maintenance	114
5.2 Greywater Usage in Gardens: Safety and Efficiency	116
5.3 Rainwater Harvesting Techniques for Gardeners	118
5.4 Scheduling Irrigation: Best Practices for Efficiency	119
5.5 Moisture Monitoring and Adjustment Strategies	122
6. ECO-FRIENDLY GARDENING PRACTICES	125
6.1 Organic Mulching: Types and Techniques for Dry Climates	125
6.2 Natural Pest Control Solutions in Arid Gardens	128
6.3 Composting in Dry Conditions: A Comprehensive Guide	129
6.4 Creating and Sustaining Biodiversity with Native Plants	131
6.5 Permaculture Techniques for the Desert Garden	133
6.6 Eco-friendly Fertilizers and Amendments for Healthy Soil	135
7. SOLVING COMMON PROBLEMS AND CHALLENGES	139
7.1 Managing Extreme Heat and Sun Exposure	140
7.2 Overcoming Poor Soil Conditions: Tips and Tricks	142

7.3 Dealing with Common Diseases and Pests in Dry Areas	144
7.4 Windbreaks and Other Solutions for Windy Areas	146
7.5 Strategies for Sloped Landscapes and Erosion Control	149
7.6 Reviving a Neglected Dry Climate Garden	151
8. ADVANCED TECHNIQUES AND FUTURE TRENDS	155
8.1 The Emerging Smart Irrigation Systems	155
8.2 Advances in Soil Science for Water Conservation	157
8.3 Reflecting on the Global Implications of Water-Smart Gardening	159
Conclusion	163
About the Author	167
Resources	169
References	171

Introduction

> "I was told - In the desert, there is nothing. I was told wrong."
>
> Unknown

I am Dian Eaton, an enthusiastic gardener in beautiful, sunny Southern California. Writing my previous books, **The Meadow Garden** and **The Pollinator Garden**, has deepened my commitment to exploring gardening ideas that both beautify and protect our environment. I am not a botanist or landscaper, but a self-taught gardener who loves learning and experimenting with new techniques. As a firm believer in sustainable, eco-friendly gardening, my latest book, **The Desert Garden**, continues that passion to show how vibrant, water-wise gardens can flourish even in arid conditions.

When I first moved to La Quinta, a desert community east of Palm Springs, California, I was captivated by the stunning landscapes and unique gardens. I was eager to create my backyard oasis, a place I could design and tend to every day. And I promised myself (and I promise you, too) there would be roses. I couldn't have a garden without roses. The thought of 120° summers didn't even bother me! But soon, I realized the truth behind the saying, "You don't know what you don't know." I had a lot to learn about the challenges of desert gardening, like high evaporation and dry soil. It was the start of an exciting adventure.

Are you new to desert areas and curious about how to start gardening in your new home? Or are you a current dry climate resident struggling to create a lush, sustainable outdoor space you can enjoy? Gardening in dry climates can seem complicated at first. However, you can achieve your gardening goals once you understand your region's land, plant, air, and water needs. With water becoming scarcer, changing how we garden is more important than ever. Despite these challenges, we can redefine beauty and sustainability in our gardens.

This guide is made for you, the Water-Wise Gardener, who wants to turn the challenges of dry climate gardening into opportunities for growth and creativity. You may have concerns like limited plant choices, unattractive landscapes, and maintenance challenges. This book addresses these concerns and offers practical strategies to overcome these issues.

The Desert Garden is not just a collection of gardening tips but a call to rethink our relationship with nature. It offers a unique blend of personal anecdotes, expert advice, and extensive research to equip you with the knowledge to create lush, water-wise gardens. High-quality photos, detailed plant profiles, and innovative techniques fill the pages, making your journey informative and visually engaging.

This book will guide you through creating a successful garden in a dry climate. It covers everything from understanding the challenges of dry climates to choosing resilient plants and using advanced water management techniques. It's a complete guide to creating a thriving desert garden that conserves resources and supports wildlife.

So, I invite you to join me in this transformative journey. Let us embrace the principles in these pages and begin crafting our sustainable gardens. Together, we can positively impact our environment and discover the joys of a water-wise, eco-friendly, vibrant garden oasis.

Whether you're a beginner or an experienced gardener, this book will be your practical guide and source of inspiration.

Have fun and be prepared for some surprises!

Welcome to **The Desert Garden**. Let's make every drop of water count and every plant a purposeful choice for a sustainable future.

ONE

Foundations of Desert Gardening

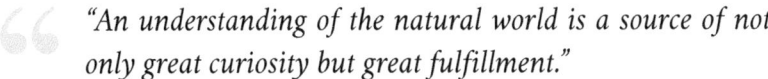

"An understanding of the natural world is a source of not only great curiosity but great fulfillment."

Sir David Attenborough

Did you know that the ancient Egyptians were some of the first to use irrigation to improve their crops in the dry Nile Valley? Like those early gardeners, today's desert gardeners face the tough challenge of growing lush gardens under the hot sun and with little rain. Gardening in these conditions requires patience, resilience, a good understanding of the environment, and creative ways to manage water. In this chapter, we'll cover the basics of desert gardening, from understanding the climate to using effective gardening strategies that save water and look great.

1.1 Defining Dry Climate and Its Impact on Gardening

Understanding Dry Climate

Dry climates have low rainfall, high evaporation rates, and often big temperature changes between day and night. These climates are found in various parts of the world like the Mediterranean regions, with hot, dry summers and mild, wet winters, and the American Southwest, where the rain shadow effects of mountain ranges create arid conditions. Gardeners in these areas face unique challenges. They must carefully consider the water needs of their plants and the timing of their gardening activities to coincide with cooler times of the day.

Impact on Gardening Practices

The lack of water in dry climates affects garden design and plant choice. Traditional green landscapes are not practical or sustainable in these areas. Gardeners should focus on saving water by choosing native or drought-resistant plants, using water-efficient systems like drip irrigation, and designing gardens that use less water. For example, adding mulch can help keep moisture in the soil, and placing taller plants strategically can provide shade to more vulnerable species.

Xeriscaping and Drought-Tolerant Plants

One effective strategy for dry climate gardening is **xeriscaping**. Xeriscaping is a method of landscaping that reduces or eliminates the need for irrigation by using drought-tolerant plants. The term comes from the Greek word "xeros," meaning "dry." This approach is ideal for creating sustainable gardens in areas with limited water.

This approach involves designing gardens requiring minimal irrigation using drought-tolerant plants and efficient water use. Xeriscaping saves water and reduces garden maintenance. Drought-tolerant (or drought-resistant) plants are well-suited for dry climates because they have deep roots that reach underground water and leaves that minimize water loss.

By learning these basic concepts, you'll gain the skills and knowledge needed for successful desert gardening. Whether you're an experienced gardener adapting to a new environment or a beginner starting your first dry-climate garden, understanding these principles is the first step to creating a thriving, sustainable garden that fits your local ecosystem. As you move forward, remember that every choice you make—like the plants you choose and your watering schedule—helps you garden more responsibly in our changing world.

1.2 The Science of Drought Tolerance in Plants

Understanding how plants adapt to dry environments is like knowing why a cactus thrives in the desert while a fern thrives in a rainforest. Each plant has developed unique features that help it survive and grow in specific conditions. For gardeners in dry climates, recognizing these adaptations is essential for creating a sustainable and beautiful garden. Let's explore how plant characteristics and genetic traits help certain plants survive in dry conditions.

Physiological Traits

Plants that do well in dry conditions have special features that help them survive. One key adaptation is deep root systems, which allow plants to reach moisture deep in the soil where it's less likely to evaporate. For example, native desert plants like the **mesquite tree** have taproots that reach deep underground to access water that shallow-rooted plants can't reach. Another common adaptation is smaller leaves, which reduce water loss. Plants like **lavender and sage** have small, needle-like leaves to minimize transpiration. Many drought-tolerant plants also have waxy or hairy leaf surfaces to prevent water loss and reflect excess sunlight, like the way sunscreen protects human skin from UV rays.

Genetic Factors

The ability of these plants to survive in dry environments is not just by chance; it's part of their genetic makeup. Drought tolerance involves many genes that control water uptake, conservation, and stress response. Advances in genetic research have helped scientists identify specific genes responsible for drought resistance. This understanding helps breeding programs introduce these traits to other plants. Modern techniques like CRISPR allow precise changes to plant genes, improving drought tolerance without the years of traditional crossbreeding. This could be a game-changer for developing crops and ornamental plants better suited to changing climate conditions.

Foundations of Desert Gardening • 19

Indicator Species

When choosing plants for a low-water garden, starting with naturally drought-tolerant species is a good idea. These plants thrive with little water and can help you decide if other plants will do well in similar conditions. **Succulents** are a great example because they store water in their thick leaves, making them perfect for dry climates. **Agave** and **aloe**, with their rosette shape, help minimize evaporation. Native grasses like **buffalo grass** and **blue grama grass** also have strong drought resistance thanks to their deep roots, allowing them to survive long dry periods. These plants save water and help prevent soil erosion, thereby maintaining the health of your garden ecosystem.

Succulents

Agave

Aloe

Buffalo Grass

Blue Grama Grass

Practical Application

Choosing the right plants for your garden isn't just about knowing their drought tolerance; it also involves testing their performance in your specific conditions. A simple way to see how plants handle water stress is to do DIY experiments like the "bucket test." In this test, you water new plants with a set amount of water in a bucket and watch how they do during a dry period. Observing how these plants cope over a dry period can give you useful information about how well they'll perform in your garden. Keeping a garden journal can also help you track the growth, health, and water needs of different plants throughout the seasons, giving you a practical guide for improving water use and plant health over time.

By using drought-resistant plants and doing strategic testing, you can create a garden that conserves water and looks beautiful and resilient. Knowing the science behind drought tolerance helps you make smart choices and aligns your gardening with sustainability and conservation principles.

1.3 Topography and Microclimates: What You Need to Know

Understanding how the layout of your garden and microclimates affects your plants is like being a weather expert for your yard. Instead of predicting the weather, you learn where your plants will thrive. Hills, valleys, walls, and even your home's building materials can change the microclimate in different parts of your garden. These small climate zones affect temperature, light, and moisture, which are important for determining what will grow well in specific areas of your landscape.

Influence of Topography

The layout of your garden, including slopes, elevation changes, and nearby structures, can greatly impact how microclimates form. For example, a garden on a slope may have different conditions at the top and bottom. Water flows downhill, so the soil at the bottom is usually moister than at the top. This is important when deciding where to plant moisture-loving plants versus those that prefer drier soil. Elevated areas might be more exposed to wind, which can cool the area and increase evaporation. Understanding these details helps you use the landscape to your advantage, creating an environment where plants can thrive.

Identifying Microclimates

To effectively manage your garden in a desert climate, begin by identifying the different microclimates. This can be as simple as observing where dew lasts the longest in the morning. You can also use garden thermometers to track temperature changes or moisture sensors to see how quickly different areas dry out after watering. Mapping these observations will help you understand your garden's microclimates, making it easier to decide where to plant each type of plant. The goal is to match each plant's needs with the natural conditions of your garden.

Leveraging Microclimates

After mapping your garden's microclimates, use this information to plant wisely. Moisture-loving plants might do well at the base of a slope where water collects. Plants that like heat and dry conditions might be best on a south-facing slope to get more sun. In shaded areas under trees or near buildings, plant shade-tolerant species that can't handle direct sunlight. Placing plants based on microclimates helps them thrive and reduces the need for extra watering and maintenance.

Using these methods, you can turn your garden into a series of habitats that meet different plants' needs. This approach saves water, reduces maintenance, and creates a thriving garden that fits the natural landscape. Spending time in your garden will help you notice its unique patterns and details, deepening your connection with nature.

1.4 Soil Types and Their Roles in Dry Climate Gardens

In dry-climate gardening, the soil is more than just dirt—it's the foundation of your garden's ecosystem. Knowing the different soil types and their characteristics can improve your gardening success in dry areas. Let's look at the common soil types in these climates—sandy, loamy, and clay—and explore how they retain water and affect garden planning and plant health.

Characteristics of Soil Types

Sandy soil has large particles and a gritty texture, which helps it drain quickly and warm up fast. This prevents waterlogging but also makes it dry out quickly and lack nutrients. In contrast, clay soil has smaller particles that hold nutrients and moisture well.

However, it drains slowly and can become waterlogged, which can suffocate plant roots if the water doesn't drain properly. Loamy soil is a mix of sandy and clay soils and is often considered the best option for gardeners. It holds moisture and nutrients while draining properly, making it ideal for many gardening situations.

Amending Soils

In dry climates, even loamy soil can have issues if not managed well because conserving water is important. You can make your garden healthier by improving the soil to hold more water and nutrients. Add organic matter like compost, well-rotted manure, or leaf mold. This helps sandy and loamy soils retain more water and nutrients, making clay soils less dense. Biochar, a type of charcoal, can also help retain water and nutrients in the soil.

Another way to improve water retention is by using vermiculite, a natural mineral that expands when heated. When mixed into the soil, vermiculite acts like a sponge, holding moisture near plant roots and releasing it slowly as needed. For clay soils, which can become compacted, adding coarse sand or gypsum can help break up the dense particles, improving drainage and allowing roots to grow better. The goal is to create soil that holds enough water but also drains well to prevent root diseases.

Soil Testing for Analysis

Soil testing is an important step in understanding what your garden needs. Simple home testing kits can give you useful information about your soil's pH level and nutrient content. You can send a soil sample to a local extension service or a professional soil lab for more detailed results. These tests can tell you about soil texture, nutrient deficiencies, and pH imbalances, helping you decide how to improve your soil. For example, if your soil test shows high alkalinity, you might need to add sulfur to lower the pH, which would help plants that prefer slightly acidic conditions.

By taking the time to understand and improve your garden soil, you create a strong foundation for your plants to thrive, even in a dry climate. Whether you have sandy, clay, or loamy soil, using the right amendments and a little effort can help you grow a lush, vibrant garden in an arid environment.

1.5 The Importance of Native Plants in Eco-Gardening

In eco-gardening, native plants are essential for making gardens resilient and sustainable. Adding native plants to your garden can help you support your local ecosystem. These plants are naturally adapted to your area's conditions, so they need less water and fewer chemical fertilizers. They also support local wildlife, making your garden more environmentally friendly.

Benefits of Native Plants

Native plants have adapted over thousands of years to the local climate and soil, making them better suited to their environment than non-native plants. They require less water and are more resistant to local diseases, reducing the need for synthetic pesticides. Native plants are essential for the local ecosystem, providing food and shelter for native birds, insects, and other wildlife. This relationship creates a healthy ecosystem that boosts biodiversity, which is important for ecological health. For example, the native purple coneflower adds color to gardens in the Midwest and provides nectar for butterflies and bees, while its seeds feed local birds during the winter.

Selecting Native Plants

Choosing the right native plants for your garden requires some planning. Start by researching the native plants in your area. You can do this by visiting local botanical gardens, consulting with regional gardening clubs, or using resources from local university extension services. When selecting plants, consider environmental factors like sunlight, soil type, and water availability. Also, consider how the plants' colors, sizes, and blooming cycles will fit into your garden's design. Each plant should complement the others, ensuring its survival and contribution to the garden's overall look.

Creating a Native Plant Garden

Creating a garden with mostly native plants can be both rewarding and beautiful. Start by designing a layout that mimics the natural landscape, such as grouping plants with similar water needs or arranging them as they grow in the wild. Use taller plants to provide shade for smaller, more delicate species, and consider adding elements like rocks or streams that are common in your local area. This approach not only conserves water and supports the ecosystem but also creates a garden that feels connected to the local environment

Sustainability Practices

Using native plants in your garden has positive effects on the environment beyond your immediate area. By creating a diverse garden, you help conserve the local environment and maintain its ecological balance. This also reduces your garden's carbon footprint by lowering the need for mowing, watering, and chemicals. Additionally, choosing native plants helps preserve genetic diversity within plant species, which can be lost due to habitat destruction and widespread commercial plant cultivation. This preservation is important because it allows these plants to adapt to changing environmental conditions and continue to thrive in the wild.

Choosing native plants for your garden isn't just about gardening; it's a way to help the environment. It's a decision to support and care for the ecosystem around you, creating a beautiful and helpful space for local wildlife. When you choose each plant, think about the beauty it adds to your garden and the life it will support, like butterflies and bees that will pollinate its flowers or birds that will eat its seeds. Each choice connects your garden more closely to nature, making it more beautiful and resilient.

1.6 Addressing Common Misconceptions About Dry Climate Gardening

People often imagine dry climate gardens as bare landscapes with only a few cacti or bushes. However, this image is far from accurate. Gardens in arid regions can be vibrant and colorful, with a variety of textures that rival any lush garden. For example, after rare rainfalls, deserts can burst into bloom with a spectacular display of flowers. These transformations show the hidden potential in seemingly desolate spaces.

Misconception: Dry Gardens are Drab

The idea that dry gardens are dull comes from not knowing about the many plants that thrive in these conditions. A dry climate garden can be as colorful as any other. Plants like the fiery red **Indian Blanket**, vivid yellow **Desert Marigold** survive and thrive in dry conditions, adding bright colors against the sandy soil.

These plants, along with textures from soft ornamental grasses like **Blue Grama** and the spiky **Agave**, create an interesting landscape. You can also add height and depth with shrubs and small trees like the **Creosote bush** and **Joshua tree**.

Blanket Flower

Desert Marigold

Creosote Bush

Joshua Tree

Misconception: Limited Plant Options

Another myth is that there aren't many plants to choose from in dry climates. While water-loving plants might not do well, there are many options for arid environments. Besides succulents and cacti, drought-tolerant grasses, perennials, and shrubs add variety to any garden. For example, **Penstemon**, with its tubular flowers, attracts hummingbirds and is aromatic, with colors from white to purple and heights up to 5 ft. Drought tolerance doesn't mean only native plants are suitable. Plants from similar climates, like **Russian Sage** from Central Asia or **Rockrose** from the Mediterranean, can also thrive, allowing you to create a globally inspired garden.

Penstemon Firebird

Russian Sage

Rockrose

Misconception: High Maintenance

While some people think dry climate gardens require high maintenance, it's important to remember that any garden requires care. However, a well-designed drought-resistant garden can reduce labor and resource use over time. Proper planning and design are essential. You can create a self-sustaining ecosystem by choosing the right plants and placing them according to their needs and the garden's microclimates. Mulching is essential because it keeps the soil moist, suppresses weeds, and reduces the need for water and upkeep. Another strategy is to group plants with similar water needs together to simplify irrigation and reduce water waste.

Misconception: Ineffective Watering Techniques

Some people criticize watering techniques in dry climates, but they can be efficient if done correctly. Drip irrigation delivers water directly to the plant's roots, reducing evaporation and runoff. This system can be automated and adjusted to each plant's needs, ensuring no water is wasted. When it's cooler, watering in the early morning or late evening also helps minimize evaporation and allows water to soak deeper into the soil, promoting healthier root growth.

Adding these elements to your garden shows the beauty and resilience of dry-climate gardening. With the proper knowledge and tools, any dry area can become a flourishing garden that conserves water and highlights the region's unique conditions. This approach makes your garden more attractive and supports sustainable living by respecting the environment's natural limits and finding beauty in balance.

TWO

Designing Your Desert Garden

> *"A collection of plants is not a landscape, any more than a list of choice words is a poem. The merit is in the design, not the material it is expressed in, and the best designs, like the best poems, make ordinary material significant by its arrangement."*
>
> — Nan Fairbrother

Stepping into the realm of desert gardening, you might find yourself surrounded by a myriad of possibilities, each more exciting than the last. It's a canvas waiting for a splash of creativity, a bit of science, and a lot of love. This chapter is dedicated to guiding you through the meticulous yet exhilarating process of designing your desert garden—a space that not only thrives under the sun but also conserves every precious drop of water.

2.1 Principles of Xeriscape Design: More Than Just Cacti

Understanding Xeriscaping

Xeriscaping is about creating landscapes that need little or no extra water from irrigation, especially useful in areas where water is scarce. It's not just about getting rid of the sprinkler system. Xeriscaping relies on seven key principles: (1) planning and design, (2) soil analysis and improvement, (3) practical turf areas, (4) appropriate plant selection, (5) efficient irrigation, (6) use of mulches, and (7) regular maintenance. Each of these helps create a garden that is both beautiful and water-efficient. By following these principles, you can turn a dry landscape into a vibrant and practical garden.

Beyond Cacti

While cacti are champions in dry environments, using only them would be like painting with one color. The beauty of xeriscaping is in its diversity. Plants like **Russian sage, Texas sage**, and certain ornamental grasses add texture, color, and movement to your garden. These drought-tolerant plants also bring surprise and delight to the landscape. For example, the vibrant purples of **lavender** attract pollinators, bringing life to your garden. The wispy elegance of **Mexican feather grass** swaying in the breeze adds a dynamic element to your space.

Designing Your Desert Garden • 33

Texas Sage

Lavender

Mexican Feather Grass

Zoning Plants According to Needs

Efficiency is key in xeriscaping, and one smart move is to zone your plants by their water needs, a strategy called hydrozoning. This involves grouping plants with similar hydration requirements to optimize irrigation. By doing this, each plant gets the right amount of water, conserving water and preventing stress from over- or under-watering. For example, you can group low-water plants like succulents and lavender together, while a slightly thirstier herb garden can be in a separate zone.

Design Aesthetics

The art of xeriscaping extends beyond plant selection and water conservation; it's also about creating a visually harmonious environment that reflects the natural beauty of the desert. To do this, use native rocks and sustainable materials that match the local landscape. These elements can be focal points or serve as pathways and borders. Using local materials looks good and reduces the carbon footprint of transporting materials from far away. In your design, aim for a balance between form and function, where every element has a purpose, whether it's providing habitat, conserving water, or enhancing the garden's overall beauty.

In designing your desert garden, remember that xeriscaping is a blend of art and science. It's an opportunity to re-envision what a garden can be—a place of beauty and sustainability deeply rooted in the principles of ecological responsibility. As you select each plant and place each stone, you're not just decorating a space; you're crafting an ecosystem that celebrates and sustains the natural world around it.

2.2 Creating Color and Contrast with Drought-Tolerant Plants

When envisioning a drought-tolerant garden, you might initially picture landscapes dominated by earth tones and greens. However, the truth is that a palette of vibrant colors and dynamic contrasts is achievable and can be wonderfully sustainable with the right plant choices. In the drought-tolerant spectrum, there's an array of plants that offer more than just resilience to dry weather—they bring bursts of joy and color that can rival any traditional garden. Let's explore some top performers that are hardy and stunning, especially for gardeners in the Western, Midwestern, and Southwestern U.S.

Designing Your Desert Garden • 35

Choosing Colorful Drought-Tolerant Plants – 15 Great Choices

The **Firecracker Penstemon**, with its vivid red blooms, is a showstopper that attracts hummingbirds and provides a bold pop of color. In the Southwest, where the sun pours down generously, the **Blue Palo Verde** thrives, its yellow flowers creating a sunny canopy. Consider the **Desert Marigold**, a resilient beauty that blankets the ground with golden hues. For a touch of the unusual, the **Red Yucca** sends up spires of coral-red flowers that seem to dance in the wind. Although not a native plant, the **Bird-of-Paradise** is another colorful, hardy, drought-tolerant plant that is easy to grow, especially in warm climates.

Firecracker Penstemon

Red Yucca

Bird-of-Paradise

Each of these plants survives and thrives with minimal water, and their colors are a testament to nature's brilliance in even the harshest conditions.

Design Techniques for Maximum Impact

Beyond choosing individual plants, using color theory in your garden can make a big difference in how your landscape looks. Color theory helps us understand how colors work together and affect the way we feel. For example, if you want to create a cool, relaxing feel in your garden, especially in hot weather, use blue and purple plants like **Lavender** and **Catmint**. These colors make the garden feel calm and cool. On the other hand, warm colors like red, orange, and yellow from plants like **Blanket Flower** and **California Poppy** bring energy and make the space feel more cozy and lively

Catmint

California Poppy

Layering and Texture

The textures and shapes of plants are important for making your garden look more interesting. For example, the soft, feathery look of ornamental grasses like **Blue Grama** looks great next to the strong, sharp shape of **Agave.** This mix of textures keeps the garden visually exciting. You create layers that add depth by placing taller plants like Joshua Trees behind shorter, softer plants. This also helps protect smaller plants from wind or too much sun, creating a better environment for them to grow.

Seasonal Planning

Seasonal planning is a smart way to keep your garden looking good all year. This means choosing plants that bloom or look their best at different times so that when one plant fades, another takes its place. Evergreens like the **Soapberry** tree or **Jojoba** bush provide green color all year, while flowers bloom seasonally to add bursts of color. Plants like the **Apache Plume** or **Desert Olive**, which have unique seed pods or bark, keep your garden interesting even in winter. The goal is to balance evergreens with seasonal plants to create a garden that's constantly changing and exciting.

Western Soapberry Tree

Jojoba Plant

Apache Plume　　　　　　　　　　New Mexico Privet (Desert Olive)

By carefully choosing plants and designing your garden with attention to color, texture, and seasonal changes, your drought-tolerant garden can become a place of endless discovery and enjoyment. It shows how nature's resilience can create beauty, proving that even in dry conditions, vibrant life can thrive. As you select and place each plant, think of the garden as a vibrant quilt of colors, textures, and forms that conserve water and celebrate the unique beauty of a dry climate garden.

2.3 To Turf or Not to Turf

Live Green Lawn

One of the biggest issues in having a live, green lawn is that it is not water-wise. Sprawling lawns with lush green grass need a lot of water to keep from burning up. As we face climate change, maintaining a drought-friendly yard is more important than ever.

Grass uses a lot of water, but if you make smart choices, you can still have a small lawn in a xeriscape. It's a matter of choosing the right type of grass. Some grasses need less water than others.

There are two major groups of grasses:

- Cool-season species like ryegrass, fescue, and bluegrass create the year-round, velvet-green look that homeowners desire, but these grasses require much more water than warm-season species.
- Warm-season species like zoysia, Bermuda, Saint Augustine, and buffalo grass do go dormant and turn brown in winter, but overseeding with ryegrass easily solves that problem.

How you maintain your lawn affects water use, too:

- Always water early in the morning when the air is cool.
- Water long enough to soak the roots.
- Water every three days in summer, once a week, or even every other week in winter.
- Keep your grass a healthy length - 1-½ to 3 inches for cool-season turf; ¾ to 1-½ inches for warm-season species.
- Occasionally rake and aerate to break up thatch and compacted soil.

In dry climates, having a live, green lawn is not a water-wise option. Artificial turf is an option with many perks. It's hassle-free and does not require watering or maintenance. However, it's not a substitute for the many benefits living plants bring to our environment.

Artificial Turf

Artificial turf is water-wise, needing no water. However, it has its downsides:

- Artificial turf is made of plastic, so while it looks like grass, it doesn't offer the same benefits.
- Turf heats your yard, sometimes reaching extreme temperatures.
- Regular cleaning is needed to stay sanitary.
- Turf is also hard and can lead to injuries.
- Turf doesn't last as long as advertised and often needs replacement in 8–10 years.
- Installation of artificial turf is expensive.
- Being plastic, artificial turf is not eco-friendly or easy to recycle.

Unlike natural grass, artificial turf doesn't cool the environment or support wildlife. It's a plastic barrier that traps heat and prevents soil from connecting with nature. This makes the ground less suitable for insects and animals, turning it more like asphalt than grass.

Turf Alternatives

When considering turf alternatives for dry climates, several options offer beauty, functionality, and low water requirements. Here are some of the best turf alternatives that are both drought-tolerant and environmentally friendly:

1. Gravel or Rock Gardens

- **Why It Works**: Gravel and rock gardens provide a clean, low-maintenance look while conserving water. For added texture, you can combine rocks with drought-resistant plants like succulents, cacti, or agave.
- **Benefits**: No watering, mowing, or fertilizing is needed. Great for arid regions.
- **Drawback**: Lacks the greenery and softness of a traditional lawn.

2. Ground Covers

- **Best Choices:**
    - **Creeping Thyme**: Low-growing, fragrant, and drought-tolerant.
    - **Lippia (Phyla nodiflora)**: Thrives in hot, dry areas and forms a green mat with small flowers.
    - **Dymondia (Silver Carpet)**: A low-maintenance option with silvery foliage.

Creeping Thyme

Lippia

Dymondia

- **Benefits**: These plants spread across the ground, creating a living lawn that needs little water.
- **Drawback**: Not ideal for heavy foot traffic, but great for visual appeal.

3. Ornamental Grasses

- **Best Choices**:
    - **Buffalo Grass**: Native to North America. It's highly drought-tolerant and can create a lawn-like appearance.

Designing Your Desert Garden • 43

- **Blue Fescue**: Adds visual interest with its blue-green hue and can handle dry conditions.
- **Purple Fountain Grass**: Decorative and hardy, perfect for accents.

Buffalo Grass

Blue Fescue

Purple Fountain Grass

- **Benefits**: Requires little water and can handle harsh climates.
- **Drawback**: It may not offer the same softness underfoot as traditional turf.

4. Native Plants and Xeriscaping

- **Why It Works**: Xeriscaping uses native plants naturally adapted to dry climates. This method often incorporates mulch, rocks, and drought-resistant species.
- **Best Choices**:
    - **Lavender, sage, rosemary,** and **succulents** like **aloe vera** or **agave**.
- **Benefits**: Extremely low water needs, supports local ecosystems, and can create a stunning, natural landscape.
- **Drawback**: It doesn't provide the same feel as grass but is great for reducing water usage.

5. Clover

- **Why It Works: Clover**, especially **microclover**, is a hardy alternative that requires far less water than grass.
- **Benefits**: Naturally fixes nitrogen in the soil, helping it stay green with minimal water.
- **Drawback**: It may not withstand heavy foot traffic in high-use areas, but it is a soft, green option.

6. Mulch or Bark

- **Why It Works**: Mulch or bark chips are excellent for creating walkable areas without water.
- **Benefits**: Prevents weed growth, retains soil moisture, and requires no water.
- **Drawback**: It doesn't have the lush green appeal of a lawn but works well in combination with drought-tolerant plants.

Choosing the suitable alternative for your climate and lifestyle allows you to create a beautiful, low-maintenance yard that requires far less water than traditional turf.

2.4 Innovative Uses of Rocks and Gravel in Design

Functional Aesthetics of Rocks

When adding rocks to your desert garden, think of them as decorative elements and functional components that enhance your space's beauty and practicality. With their rugged textures and natural colors, rocks blend seamlessly into a desert landscape, offering a look that is both rustic and elegant. Beyond their visual appeal, rocks serve practical purposes. For example, on cooler desert nights, rocks can absorb heat from the sun during the day and release it slowly after sunset, creating microclimates that help maintain stable temperatures around your plants. This natural temperature regulation is important for plant health, especially in spring and fall when night temperatures can drop unexpectedly.

Rocks can also create natural-looking boundaries and edges in your garden, eliminating the need for artificial barriers. These boundaries help organize the space visually and manage foot traffic by guiding visitors along designated paths and away from more sensitive plants. Placing larger rocks strategically can help control erosion by anchoring the soil in sloped areas and reducing runoff during heavy rain. When placed thoughtfully, rocks are more than just decoration; they help structure and protect your garden.

Gravel as a Ground Cover

Gravel is a versatile addition to a desert garden. It helps with moisture retention by covering the soil and reducing evaporation, which is essential in areas where water is scarce. Gravel also acts as a barrier between the sun and the soil, keeping the ground moist longer after watering or rain. It suppresses weeds by preventing seeds from reaching the soil and germinating, saving time and effort in weeding.

Gravel also has aesthetic benefits. It comes in various colors, from deep red lava rock to pale white marble chips and different textures, allowing you to match or contrast with the plants in your garden. This versatility can make green leaves pop and flowers stand out against the neutral background. Gravel pathways create a clean, cohesive look that makes your garden appear larger and more open, guiding the eye smoothly across the space.

Creating Rock Gardens

Designing a rock garden is like painting a landscape on canvas, except your medium is the earth itself, and your elements are stones and plants. Start by selecting a spot in your garden with plenty of sunlight, as most rock garden plants thrive in full sun. If your chosen area isn't naturally well-drained—a must for rock gardens—consider elevating it slightly or incorporating a mix of sand and gravel into the soil to improve drainage.

Gravel ground cover with cacti, rocks, and Palo Verde Tree

When choosing plants, choose drought-resistant ones that can thrive in rocky soil. Good options include **sedum**, **creeping thyme**, and some cacti and succulents, as they need little soil and can handle dry conditions. Plant them in clusters and pockets for a natural look and consider how the colors and textures will work with the rocks. The final arrangement should feel like a balanced mix of stone and plants, with each enhancing the beauty of the other.

Sedum

Creeping Thyme

Incorporating Boulders

Boulders are the sentinels of the garden, grounding the landscape with their substantial presence. When integrating larger stones, consider them as focal points and functional elements. Positioned strategically, a boulder can serve as a natural seat, warming under the sun and offering a resting spot. A well-placed boulder can break up the space in more extensive gardens, drawing the eye and creating visual interest.

In addition to seating, consider using boulders to anchor the corners of your property or line the sides of a gravel pathway. This adds definition and creates a sense of boundary. The goal is to place these large rocks to look natural, as if wind and water had settled them there over time. This might mean burying part of the boulder or positioning it at an angle like it had rolled down a mountain stream. This creates a feeling of stability and rugged beauty, connecting your garden to the natural history of the surrounding landscape.

Using these elements, your desert garden becomes a place of innovation and imagination, where rocks and gravel play more than a supporting role—they star in a beautiful and sustainable landscape.

2.5 Shade Planning: Maximizing Comfort and Plant Health

Importance of Shade

Managing a desert garden's bright sun and intense heat means carefully adding shade. While sunlight is good for plant growth, too much can cause stress, burning, and quick moisture loss. Adding shade is important because it shields plants from the harsh midday sun and creates a cooler environment to help them stay healthy. This approach isn't just about comfort; it's about making sure plants and people thrive during the hottest part of summer.

Natural vs. Artificial Shade

In garden design, you can create shade with natural elements like trees and shrubs or artificial structures like **pergolas** and **shade cloths**. Each option has benefits, depending on your garden's needs and preferences. Natural shade from **deciduous trees** or **tall shrubs** relieves the sun, offers habitats for wildlife, and improves air quality. Their leaves capture moisture and help cool the air. On the other hand, artificial structures like pergolas provide immediate shade without the wait for trees to grow and can be placed to make outdoor spaces more usable. You can add climbing plants like wisteria or grapevines to pergolas for extra shade that changes with the seasons.

Strategic Placement for Shade

Placing shade elements strategically is crucial for making them effective. Consider how the sun moves across your garden and identify areas that receive intense midday heat. These spots are ideal for shade structures or plants. For example, placing a pergola over a seating area can create a comfortable retreat from the sun, making it a great spot for relaxing or socializing. Similarly, planting a tall shrub near a vegetable garden can protect sensitive veggies from too much sun, which can help them grow better. The key is to balance sun and shade so that each plant gets the right amount of light it needs to thrive.

Shade planning is an art that balances beauty with practicality, creating attractive and comfortable spaces. It lets you enjoy your garden even on the hottest days and helps your plants thrive in the harsh conditions of a desert climate. By carefully using natural and artificial shade and choosing the right plants for each shaded area, you can create a cool oasis, inviting and vibrant garden filled with life and comfort.

2.6 Paths and Walkways: Functional and Water-Smart Solutions

Designing for Accessibility and Flow

When creating paths in your desert garden, making them useful and attractive is essential. Paths do more than just guide where you walk; they help shape how the garden feels and show off key areas. The design should feel natural, leading you through the garden quickly while being practical. For example, wider paths can fit a garden cart or allow people with mobility aids to move around comfortably, ensuring everyone can enjoy the garden without trouble.

Materials Selection

Choosing suitable materials for your garden paths is essential, especially in dry areas where water-saving matters. Materials that let water soak into the ground are the best choice. They help reduce water runoff and make rain or irrigation more effective. Decomposed granite is a good option because it's firm to walk on and lets water reach plant roots. Crushed gravel or packed sand also provides a solid surface while allowing water to flow through, stopping puddles and helping water get to where it's needed.

Incorporating Runoff Solutions

Including solutions for water runoff in your garden paths can help improve how well your garden uses water. For example, sloping paths slightly toward plant beds can guide water to the plants, making the most of rainfall or watering. This saves water and gives plants extra moisture, cutting down the need for more irrigation. Another option is adding drainage systems under the paths to catch extra water and send it to drier areas of the garden. This is especially useful for gardens on a slope, where runoff happens more often.

Aesthetic Integration

Integrating paths into your garden design should feel as natural and inviting as the plants themselves. You can line the edges of your pathways with low, drought-tolerant plants like **creeping thyme** or **blue fescue**. These plants soften the edges of the gravel or stone and add color and life, making the path blend seamlessly into the garden. For evening ambiance and safety, add solar-powered lights along the pathway to provide a gentle, eco-friendly glow. This subtle lighting highlights pathways and key features and creates a serene atmosphere to enjoy the garden after sunset.

2.7 Mulching Techniques Specific to Dry Climates

Benefits of Mulching

In desert gardening, mulch is vital for conserving water for, stopping weeds, and keeping the soil at the right temperature. It works like a shield for the soil, protecting it from the hot sun and reducing water loss, which is crucial in dry areas. Mulch also keeps the soil cooler during the day and warmer at night, which is helpful in cooler desert nights. Plus, blocking sunlight prevents weeds from growing, so you spend less time pulling them out.

Choosing the Right Mulch

When picking mulch for your desert garden, think about how it works and looks. **Gravel mulch**, often used in xeriscaping, reflects heat and holds little water, making it great for cacti and succulents. It also gives your garden a natural, rough look. **Bark chips** are better for areas where you want to keep moisture and have a softer, more organic feel. They add nutrients to the soil as they break down but must be replaced more often. **Decomposed granite** is another good option. It's long-lasting, looks earthy, and provides good drainage. Each type of mulch has pros and cons, so your choice should fit your plants' needs and the style you want for your garden.

Application Techniques

Applying mulch correctly is important for getting the most benefit. Start by removing any weeds before adding mulch to help stop new ones from growing. A two to three-inch layer of mulch is usually enough to keep in moisture and block weeds. But don't pile mulch right up against plant stems or tree trunks, as it can trap moisture and cause rot. In areas with gravel or stones, you can use landscape fabric underneath to help stop weeds while still letting water and air through. Make sure the mulch is spread evenly and reaches out to the edges of your plants to help save water.

Maintenance Tips

Taking care of your mulch is as important as choosing and applying it. Organic mulches, like bark chips, break down over time, so they need to be replaced to keep working well. Check the mulch regularly and add more if needed to keep the right thickness. For inorganic mulches, like gravel, watch for areas where it gets packed down or moved by wind or water, and rake it back into place. Be sure to pull any weeds that appear so they don't spread. Proper upkeep helps your mulch keep your garden healthy and looking good.

Using mulch in your desert garden does more than help your plants, it also makes your garden more sustainable and beautiful. Mulch is a protective layer that saves water, improves the soil, and helps your garden grow strong. Creating a sustainable desert garden is an ongoing process, with each step adding to the success of a healthy and balanced garden.

2.8 The Desert Meadow Garden

Creating a Meadow Garden in Dry-Climates

Creating a low-maintenance, drought-tolerant wildflower meadow garden is an exciting adventure. When all your other gardening activities are implemented, established, and not needing as much attention, you may be tempted by the lure of a meadow garden. A meadow is a natural garden requiring less planning and maintenance and using only native plants to enrich the environment. It is a garden created to entice birds, butterflies, and bees with rich native plants and colorful patches of wildflowers. It is a garden teeming with activity. Your oasis. Every day.

Designing Your Desert Garden • 55

A small meadow garden filled with native plants and wildflowers helps strengthen your outdoor spaces' ecosystem. More variety in plants and flowers also helps attract beneficial pollinators such as bees, butterflies, hummingbirds, and small mammals. This is especially important for some critters dealing with habitat loss from human activity.

A meadow can fit anywhere: a small corner of your yard, along a fence, around a fountain, or even in a planter on your porch. It doesn't have to be big. Meadows are informal, low-maintenance gardens that grow and change over time. Let them develop naturally and enjoy the process as they evolve.

What is a Meadowscape?

"Meadowscape" is the overall term referring to a landscape design that emulates and promotes the growth of a natural meadow, whether a prairie-sized meadow or a small meadow garden. Unlike traditionally manicured lawns or gardens, meadowscapes prioritize a mix of native grasses, wildflowers, and perennials that flourish together. Many gardeners today are removing their lawns and creating meadow gardens with wildflowers and native plants.

In dry-climate and desert regions, we plan gardens with drought-tolerant and native plants. The main objective of dry-climate gardening is saving water. We also focus on the maintenance needs of the landscapes and gardens we create.

In a meadowscape, or the smaller version, a meadow garden, gardeners focus on working with nature, following her leads, and giving her the soil and the plants and grasses she needs in the hopes that we can support the environment and mimic the natural cycle of life. In all of this, there is change every day.

A meadow garden can be as large or small as you like. In the front yard, you could plant a small strip of wildflowers alongside your drought-tolerant plants to attract pollinators and add more life to the area. Or, you could transform your backyard into a larger meadow, creating a natural haven for wildlife. As a gardener, you don't always need to control everything—sometimes, letting nature take the lead is more rewarding.

Creating Your Meadow Garden

Now that you know the benefits and challenges of meadowscaping, it's time to learn how to create one. This chapter will provide a step-by-step guide. Meadowscaping isn't just about tossing seeds and waiting for plants to grow—it requires time, planning, and some upkeep.

Decide on Seeds or Plants

First, decide whether to use seeds or plants. Seeds are cheaper but take time to grow, while live plants are more expensive but are established quickly. Choose native species, as they are better suited to the local environment and support birds and insects. Avoid "meadow in a can" products containing non-native plants.

Determine the Perfect Location for Your Meadowscape

When choosing a spot for your meadowscape, pick an area that won't be disturbed by foot traffic. It should get enough sunlight and have good drainage for healthy growth. If you need a traditional lawn for high-traffic areas, you can still include one. You could also add a path with pavers or gravel.

Determine the Perfect Location for Your Meadowscape

You don't need a big yard for a meadowscape. Even a small pollinator garden can benefit your yard and the environment. Focus on growing native wildflowers and grasses to attract wildlife and bring ecological benefits.

Familiarize Yourself With Local Rules

Research any neighborhood or homeowners' association rules about yard appearance, including mowing requirements. If height restrictions apply, try low-maintenance grasses like creeping or clumping fescue that require less mowing.

Prepare the Site

Removing an existing lawn can be challenging. You can dig it up, cover it with cardboard and compost (sheet-mulching), or use a plastic sheet to kill the grass (solarizing). After removal, check the soil's pH, fertility, and drainage, and add any necessary amendments for healthy plant growth.

Select the Right Time to Plant

Most gardeners plant seeds in summer, but for a meadowscape, it's better to plant in fall or early spring. Cooler temperatures and moist soil help your plants get established.

Add Hardscaping

Create pathways in your garden using gravel or stones, which are easy and efficient. Ensure your hardscape design allows easy access to all parts of the garden.

Select Your Preferred Plants

Selecting your plants should be fun as you envision your garden. Start with ornamental grasses as the foundation, then add native perennials and wildflowers. Consider including one or two shrubs for variety. Remember, your meadowscape will be smaller than a wild meadow. Good options for ornamental grasses include Silver Grass, Cape Rush, and Blue Fescue. For native grasses, try Switchgrass, Blue grama, and Little Bluestem.

Monitor the Presence of Any Invasive Species

Check your meadow regularly for weeds or invasive plants, especially when your plants are young. Remove any weeds to ensure your native grasses and wildflowers get enough nutrients, water, and sunlight. Adding mulch can help prevent weed growth.

Help Your Plants Get Established in the Meadowscape

Monitor your plants' needs to help them grow in your meadowscape. Seeds take time to sprout, so consider planting mature plants for quicker results. During the first year, water your plants regularly. Once their roots are established, they will need less water.

Make Your Yard Wildlife-Friendly

Plan your meadow to support wildlife. It can host beneficial insects, birds, and other animals, helping keep pests and diseases away. Add features like bird baths or bee cups for drinking and bathing to attract wildlife, as well as fallen logs for nesting and shelter.

Maintain Your Meadowscape

Your meadowscape needs occasional care, such as weeding, mulching, and pruning. Some gardeners mow once a year to keep it tidy and promote new growth. Be mindful of when to cut or mow to prevent overgrowth. Water your garden in the early morning so the sun can dry the plants, reducing the risk of disease.

No matter the size and shape of your meadowscape, you are doing a great job as long as it provides you with a beautiful yard or patio and wildlife habitat.

Establishing a meadowscape requires a financial investment, physical preparation, and ongoing maintenance. Despite the effort, meadow gardens can be stunning and rewarding, offering a sustainable and natural alternative to traditional landscaping.

THREE

Plant Selection and Care

 "The garden suggests there might be a place where we can meet nature halfway."

Michael Pollan

Cacti and succulents have evolved to survive in low water conditions and extreme temperatures over thousands of years, bringing artistic beauty and dimension to dry-climate gardens. By choosing these resilient plants, you can create a vibrant, water-saving landscape. This chapter will guide you in selecting hardy and visually appealing plants, making your garden thrive, whether you're a seasoned gardener or just starting out.

3.1 Cacti and Succulents: Choosing the Right Plants for Your Garden

Variety and Versatility of Succulents

Cactus plants, many native to the Southwest and Mexico, offer various striking forms and textures. These plants come in incredible shapes, from towering spires and broad, flat paddles to squat, round cylinders. What you're seeing are the fleshy, water-storing stems of desert plants that have evolved to survive extreme heat and drought by holding onto precious rainwater from the winter months. This makes them ideal for dry, low-water landscapes. You can use their unique shapes and colors to add bold, sculptural elements to your garden. They are like natural garden sculptures that create a sense of drama or whimsy, depending on your design.

Succulents and Cacti

There is much more to xeriscaping than adding succulents and cacti. But that doesn't mean you can't use these spectacular species to your advantage.

Succulents and **cacti** are not the same thing, but they are related. Think of cacti as a special type of succulent with their own distinct characteristics.

- **Succulents** are a broad category of plants that have the ability to store water in their thick leaves, stems, or roots. Their look is determined by the arrangement and shape of their leaves, in a wide variety of forms, including rosettes, trailing vines, and compact clusters.
- **Cacti** are a specific group of succulents, many of which are native to the Southwest and Mexico, that have unique adaptations like round indentations along their stems,

called "areoles", from which spring the spines. They often have a more distinct and recognizable shape, from towering spires and broad, flat paddles to squat, round cylinders.

Cacti and succulents naturally thrive in open, airy spaces, so give them plenty of room to spread out, especially the larger varieties. Despite their rugged appearance, they require very little water. They do best with well-draining sandy or gritty soil, to prevent root rot. Cacti and succulents also do well in pots, making them versatile for smaller spaces like patios or balconies. Their low-maintenance needs and ability to withstand tough conditions make them a fantastic choice for a vibrant, water-wise landscape.

Cacti

Succulents

Benefits of Cactus & Succulents

Creating a drought-tolerant garden with cactus and succulents has many benefits:

- **Low Maintenance:** These easy-care plants require minimal watering due to their ability to store water in their leaves or stems.
- **Diverse Shapes and Sizes:** They come in various shapes, sizes, and colors, making them versatile for different aesthetics.

- **Indoor and Outdoor Options:** You can grow them indoors or outdoors, adding greenery to any space.
- **Adaptability:** Cacti and succulents can thrive in arid conditions and resist neglect.

Succulents as Houseplants

Succulents are popular houseplants because they're attractive and easy to care for. They've been grown indoors since the 17th century and need minimal upkeep when properly potted. Succulents are very adaptable houseplants and will thrive in various indoor conditions. Over-watering and associated infections are the leading cause of succulent death for most plant owners.

Succulent Art

Their popularity has given rein to many designs in potting and placement, including living wall succulents, framed succulents, training ceiling succulents, and succulents in teapots and cups. Succulents have become a new art form.

Choosing the Right Succulents for Your Garden - 12 Popular Best Choices

There are over 2,000 species of succulents and cacti in the world. All the plants listed below grow well in California, Arizona, Texas, Florida, or other areas in USDA zones 9-11. Here are 12 interesting and popular choices for a Southwestern dry-climate garden:

1. Golden Barrel Cactus (Echinocactus grusonii)

The golden barrel cactus makes an excellent focal point in a garden. Its unique round shape and vibrant golden color stand out among the rocks and other plants. The golden barrel cactus is a low-maintenance plant that thrives in rocky environments. Its spiky texture adds an interesting contrast to the smoothness of the rocks, creating a visually striking composition.

Mature Size: 2 feet tall, 2 feet wide.

Flower Color: Yellow

2. Euphorbia Firesticks (Euphorbia tirucalli)

The Euphorbia firestick ('Sticks on Fire') is the most popular choice for high-end rock gardens. These stunning succulents have vibrant, fiery orange and red stems that resemble flickering flames, creating a striking visual impact in any rock garden.

Mature Size: 30 in. tall, 10 in. wide.

Flower Color: Yellow

3. Black Rose (Aeonium arboreum 'Zwartkop')

The Black Rose is a stunning choice for rock gardens. This unique succulent features rosettes of dark burgundy or almost black leaves. When used in rock gardens, the deep, dark foliage of black rose is sure to make a statement in any rock garden.

Mature Size: 5 ft. tall, 3 ft. wide.

Flower Color: Yellow

4. African Milk Tree (Euphorbia trigona rubra)

The African milk tree is an excellent choice for a rock garden due to its tall, branching stems with vibrant red or purple coloring, which add a pop of color to any rock garden. The Rubra, or Royal Red variety, is known for its vibrant red color, which develops late in the growing season. When used in rock gardens, the African milk tree creates a visually striking contrast against the neutral tones of the rocks, making it a focal point of interest.

Mature Size: 9 ft. tall, 2 ft. wide

Flower Color: Pink, Red

5. Brazilian Blue Cactus (Pilosocereus azureus)

The Brazilian Blue Cactus is a stunning cactus species highly sought after for its striking blue-green coloration. This cactus is popular in landscaping and gardens due to its unique appearance which adds a pop of color and interest to any outdoor space. It is relatively low maintenance, thrives in dry, arid conditions and is quite resilient to drought.

Mature Size: 12 ft. tall, 4 ft. wide

Flower Color: White

6. Aeonium Mardi Gras

The Aeonium Mardi Gras is a popular choice for landscaping and gardens due to its eye-catching variegated foliage, featuring vibrant shades of green, pink, and white. Aeonium Mardi Gras is low maintenance, thrives in well-draining soil and moderate sunlight, and brings a touch of joy and flair to the surroundings.

Mature Size: 4 in. tall, 6 in. wide

Flower Color: White, Yellow

7. Aloe Vera (Aloe barbadensis miller)

The Aloe Vera is a versatile and popular plant known for its various medicinal and skincare properties. It features long, thick, succulent leaves filled with a gel-like substance that is widely used for its healing properties. Aloe Vera is a highly sought-after plant for gardens and is low maintenance,  requiring minimal watering and sunlight. It is an excellent choice for those looking to add a touch of greenery that also serves practical purposes like soothing sunburns and promoting skin health.

Mature Size: 3 ft. tall, 2 ft. wide.

Flower Color: Yellow, red, orange

8. Color Guard Yucca (Yucca filamentosa)

Yucca 'Color Guard' is a stunning and resilient low-maintenance plant perfect for adding a pop of color to your garden. This variegated yucca boasts striking yellow and green sword-shaped leaves adorned with curly, thread-like filaments.

Mature Size: 3 ft. Tall, 4 ft. wide

Flower Color: Creamy White

9. Golden Saguaro (Neobuxbaumia polylopha)

The golden saguaro is a striking cactus species known for its unique golden-yellow spines that set it apart from traditional saguaros. This cactus is low maintenance, requiring minimal care and thriving in arid conditions with occasional watering. Its distinctive golden hue and impressive size make it a standout addition to any desert landscape, adding a touch of elegance and uniqueness with its golden spines.

Mature Size: 42 ft. tall, 14 in. wide

Flower Color: Scarlet (Dark red)

10. Blue Chalk Sticks (Senecio mandraliscae)

The Blue chalk sticks are the most popular ground cover plant for rock gardens in Southern California. These succulents have beautiful blue-gray cylindrical leaves that resemble chalk sticks, hence their name. Their vibrant blue color really stands out and creates a striking contrast with other rock garden plants. Not only do they add a pop of color, but they also have a trailing habit, which makes them perfect for cascading over the edges of rocks or walls.

Mature Size: 18 in. tall, 24 in. wide

Flower Color: Dull White

11. Gollum Jade (Crassula ovata 'Gollum')

The Gollum jade is a popular choice for rock gardens. Enjoy the natural bonsai-like charm of this Jade plant with its visible branches. These perennial succulents have elongated tubular leaves that resemble the character Gollum from "The Lord of the Rings." Their quirky appearance adds a touch of whimsy and charm to any rock garden.

Mature Size: 3 ft. tall, 2 ft. wide

Flower Color: White

12. Desert Rose (Adenium obesum)

The Desert Rose is not a rose but a popular succulent known for its bright flowers and bonsai-like appearance, making it a favorite for gardens and landscaping. The plant's popularity stems from its stunning display of colorful blooms in pink, red, and white shades. Its striking beauty adds an exotic feel to any outdoor space. It is also prized as an indoor plant. The Desert Rose thrives in dry conditions and resists pests, making it perfect for adding elegance and color without much care.

Mature Size: 9 ft. tall, 5 ft. wide

Flower Color: Pink, Red, White

Succulents are often the first plants we think of for drought-tolerant gardening, and for good reason. These hardy plants can handle dry conditions because their thick, fleshy leaves store water. But succulents do more than survive; they also add beauty and versatility to any garden.

Design Tips with Succulents

Succulents are great for any garden, from traditional beds to creative designs. For a modern look, try a vertical succulent garden to save space and add greenery to walls. Rockeries, where succulents grow among stones, mimic their natural habitat and look artistic. Even simple borders benefit from succulents' varied shapes and colors, which can define paths and edges.

By learning about different succulents and drought-resistant plants, you can create a garden that's both easy to care for and beautiful. Consider how each plant fits with your existing garden and helps build a sustainable, vibrant space that shows off your style and saves water.

3.2 Deep Dive into Desert Perennials: Long-Lived Beauty

Characteristics of Desert Perennials

Desert perennials are tough plants that need minimal care and thrive where others might struggle under the harsh sun. These plants are survivors; they have adapted over generations to make the most of limited moisture and poor soil in their native habitats. Their success comes from features like deep roots that reach for moisture and thick, waxy leaves that reduce water loss. This resilience makes them ideal for your garden, especially if you want a space that's both sustainable and beautiful.

Popular Perennials for Dry Climates

Bougainvillea, **Agastache,** and **Penstemon** are three standout desert perennials known for their drought tolerance and striking beauty.

Bougainvillea can be grown on trellises, fences, or walls or pruned into a shrub or tree form and is a significant pollinator attractor.

Bougainvillea

Agastache, or hummingbird mint, has spiky flowers and aromatic leaves that attract pollinators and add color to the sandy desert landscape.

Agastache

Penstemon features bell-shaped blossoms in various colors, from vibrant reds to deep purples, adding depth and contrast to any dry garden. These plants survive and bring dynamic beauty to their surroundings, proving that water-wise gardens can be lush and colorful.

Penstemon

Planting and Spacing Best Practices

When adding perennials to your garden, follow good planting and spacing practices for the best growth and blooms. Know the mature size of each plant to avoid overcrowding, which can cause competition for water and nutrients. A good rule is to space plants at least as far apart as they grow tall. This helps with air circulation to prevent disease and gives roots enough room to spread. Use compost to enrich the soil when planting, helping your perennials start strong and grow quickly with less maintenance.

Companion Planting for Perennials

Companion planting is an age-old strategy that involves placing plants together for mutual benefit. With desert perennials, choose companions that can handle harsh conditions without competing too much for resources. For example, pairing **Penstemon** with native grasses like **Blue Grama** creates a harmonious display that controls erosion and maintains soil health. The grasses have fine roots that help prevent soil erosion, while Penstemon's deeper roots bring up nutrients, benefiting both plants. You can also include leguminous plants like **Lupines**, which add nitrogen to the soil and enrich it for nearby plants. This method enhances your garden's visual appeal and creates a healthy, sustainable ecosystem where plants support each other's growth.

Lupines

Using desert perennials in your garden is the most beneficial way to create a sustainable and resilient environment that highlights the unique beauty of drought-tolerant plants. As you choose and arrange each plant, consider the balance of colors, textures, and heights and how they benefit each other and the entire garden. This thoughtful approach not only improves the beauty and health of your garden but also makes your gardening an act of environmental stewardship, conserving resources while providing a refuge for native wildlife and plants. By cultivating these perennials, you craft a living landscape that showcases adaptation and beauty, demonstrating nature's resilience.

3.3 The Perennial Desert Rose

The Rose Garden

I promised you a rose garden, and here it is. **Yes, you can definitely have roses in a desert climate.** It will take some work and patience, but you're a **Gardener;** you can do this!

Roses are perennials and are often considered the most beautiful flowers in any garden, but many people think they are hard to grow, prone to diseases, and require expert skills to prune. In reality, roses are no more challenging to grow than other plants. The key to success is choosing the suitable variety, the right location, and preparing the soil as you would for any shrub. With these steps, your roses will thrive.

Drought-tolerant roses should be your preferred choice if you live in a dry or desert region. These varieties can handle hot, dry climates with minimal water.

Roses can survive in dry climates, but they need proper care and watering, especially during their first few years:

- **Watering**: Water roses deeply and regularly, especially during hot weather. Roses in pots may need daily watering.
- **Soil type**: Check the soil's pH level and adjust accordingly. Sandy soil dries out quickly, so mulch and a moisture meter are used to monitor water levels.
- **Mulching**: Add a 3–4 inch layer of organic mulch to reduce evaporation and keep roots cool.

- **Planting**: Roses generally need 6 to 8 hours of sunlight daily. In arid zones, however, some partial shade is considered during the hottest part of the day.
- **Rose type**: Some roses, like Chinas, noisettes, and teas, are drought-resistant and require less maintenance.

Drought-Tolerant Roses

There are many **drought-tolerant roses** to choose from. Trust your nurseryman's advice on your selection. Here are **five** of the most popular drought-tolerant rose varieties that thrive in dry-climate environments:

1. Lady Banks' Rose (Rosa banksiae)

Description: A vigorous, thornless climbing rose, Lady Banks' rose produces small, delicate yellow or white blooms in clusters.

- **Water Needs**: Very low once established.
- **Notable Features**: Extremely hardy and **heat and drought-tolerant**. It blooms once in spring and then provides attractive green foliage for the rest of the year.

Lady Banks' Rose

***Special Note*:**

In Tombstone, Arizona, there is a 139-year-old White Lady Banksia Rose, named **the largest rose tree ever grown.** The White Lady Banksia Rose is covered with clusters of miniature white tea roses. You can often smell the rose perfume in the breeze a block or two away. The rose was a gift from Scotland to a young Scottish couple who had moved to Tombstone to start their married life. They eventually established the Rose Tree Inn and the Rose Tree Museum.

Tombstone's Rose Tree was made famous when Robert Ripley included it in his widely syndicated column "Believe It or Not." The World's Largest Rose Tree is also listed in the Guinness Book of World Records, and its status has never been challenged. The World's Largest Rose Tree is celebrated every spring with The Rose Festival.

Tombstone's White Lady Banksia Rose Tree

2. Iceberg Rose (Rosa 'Iceberg')

- **Description**: One of the most popular rose varieties, the Iceberg rose has clusters of pure white blooms.

Iceberg Rose

- **Water Needs**: **Heat-tolerant**, with minimal water needs once established.
- **Notable Features**: Iceberg is disease-resistant and blooms continuously, making it both beautiful and **resilient in arid regions**

3. Knock Out Roses (Rosa 'Radrazz')

- **Description**: Known for their hardiness and vibrant red, pink, or yellow blooms, Knock Out roses are widely regarded as easy-care roses. These tough roses can handle the heat in arid climates.

Knockout Rose

- **Water Needs**: Require occasional deep watering but are **highly drought-tolerant** once established
- **Notable Features**: They resist many common rose diseases and thrive in **full sun**.

4. Belinda's Dream (Rosa 'Belinda's Dream')

- **Description**: A disease-resistant shrub rose with large, fragrant pink flowers.
- **Water Needs**: Low water needs after establishment.
- **Notable Features**: Its thick, glossy foliage and large blooms make it ideal for **heat and drought tolerance.**

Belinda's Dream Rose

My Belinda's Dream Rose Tree under the shade of a Pepper Tree

5. Austrian Copper Rose (Rosa foetida 'Bicolor')

- **Description**: This historic rose produces striking, copper-orange and yellow single blooms.
- **Water Needs**: **Extremely drought-tolerant** once established.
- **Notable Features**: This rose is known for its ability to thrive in poor soil and extreme heat, making it **ideal for desert areas.**

Austrian Copper Rose

These rose varieties are ideal for the dry, hot Southwestern desert. They require minimal water while providing stunning flowers and beauty to any garden. To further ensure their success, it's essential to plant them in well-drained soil and water deeply but infrequently. Mulching around the base will also help retain moisture and cool the roots during extreme heat.

3.4 Annuals and Biennials That Thrive in Arid Zones

Benefits of Annuals and Biennials

In a desert garden, annuals and biennials are like sparklers—bright and short-lived. They add excitement by blooming for a season or two, changing the look of your garden each year. This allows you to try out new plants and designs, keeping your garden fresh. These short-lived plants are helpful because they quickly fill empty spaces and add color and texture to your garden. For example, picture the bright yellows of **California poppies** lighting up your spring garden or the deep blues of **bluebells** cooling down the summer air.

Selecting Suitable Species

To choose the right annuals and biennials for dry conditions, look for plants that can thrive with less water. For example, **Zinnias** love full sunlight and can handle heat well, offering colors like vivid pinks and rich oranges. **California poppies** are drought-tolerant and often reseed themselves, bringing back their golden blooms year after year. **Snapdragons** add height and come in various colors, while **Dusty Miller**, with its silver leaves, provides a cool contrast to the warmer tones typical of dry gardens.

Zinnias   Snapdragons

Dusty Miller

Incorporating Annuals into Garden Design

Adding annuals and biennials to your garden is like adding accessories to an outfit—they enhance and complement your garden's permanent features. Many of these plants can handle dry conditions but still need some water and shade. Use them to fill gaps left by plants that are dormant or done blooming. This keeps your garden looking full and lively throughout the growing season. For example, you can use annuals like **Cosmos** or **Marigolds** to add color and mark the seasons. Imagine a garden corner brightening up with marigolds' reds and oranges in the fall, adding warmth as the weather cools.

Cosmos

Desert Marigold

Care Tips for Annuals and Biennials

Caring for annuals and biennials requires some attention to keep them thriving. Watering needs can vary; some may need regular moisture, especially during the summer, to keep blooming. Check the soil regularly to ensure it's moist but not waterlogged. Mulching around these plants can help retain moisture and keep the roots cool. Most annuals need to be replanted each year, although some, like **California poppies**, might self-seed and come back on their own. Biennials, such as **foxgloves**, usually bloom in their second year, so plan your garden to have some blooming each year. Rotating these plants also helps prevent soil nutrient depletion, keeping your garden healthy and vibrant.

Foxglove

By welcoming the short-lived beauty of annuals and biennials, you bring a sense of change and renewal to your garden. Each season offers a new palette and a chance to refresh your space. These plants fill the gaps between the more permanent features of your garden, creating a constantly changing and engaging landscape. When you plant seeds or young plants, you're not just gardening;

you're preparing for a colorful display that will unfold season after season.

3.5 Trees and Shrubs for Dry Conditions: A Detailed Guide

Selecting Trees and Shrubs

When planning your dry climate garden, the trees and shrubs you choose can greatly impact its look, ecological balance, and functionality. Selecting the right ones means understanding how well they fit your local climate, especially their ability to thrive with little water. Native species are usually the best choices because they naturally adapt to local climate and soil conditions, which reduces the need for extra watering and care. For example, in the Southwestern United States, native plants like the **Mesquite tree** or the **Creosote bush** are ideal for local gardens because they have evolved to excel in hot, dry conditions. Other choices include: **Sweet Acacia, Desert Willow, Palo Verde, California Pepper Tree, Texas Ebony and Crepe Myrtle.** These plants have deep root systems to access scarce water, and their leaves often have waxy coatings to minimize water loss.

Mesquite Tree

Sweet Acacia

Plant Selection and Care • 85

Desert Willow

Palo Verde

California Pepper Tree

Crepe Myrtle

Benefits of Including Trees and Shrubs

Adding trees and shrubs to your dry garden has many benefits. They provide essential habitats and food for local wildlife, supporting biodiversity. For example, trees like the **Palo Verde** offer lush, green canopies and vibrant yellow blooms that attract bees and birds, making your garden lively for wildlife. Trees and shrubs can change your garden's microclimate by providing shade, reducing soil temperature, and slowing moisture evaporation, which helps conserve water. Their roots also stabilize the soil and prevent erosion by wind and water.

Planting Techniques for Success

Planting larger plants like trees and shrubs requires careful planning to ensure they stay healthy and last long. Start by checking your garden's soil type and drainage, as most trees and shrubs need well-draining soil. If your soil holds water or is compacted, try mixing in sand or organic matter to improve it. When planting, dig a hole twice as wide as the root ball but no deeper, as planting too deep can suffocate the roots. After planting, make a basin around the base to direct water to the roots and encourage deep root growth. This helps create a strong root system that can access underground water, which is important for survival in dry conditions.

Ongoing Care and Pruning

Caring for your plants, especially young ones, is key to their success in your garden. Water them regularly, adjusting for the season and their age, to help them adjust to their new home. Mature trees and shrubs need less frequent watering but benefit from deeper watering to encourage roots to grow deep rather than staying near the surface. Pruning is also important for plant health and shape. Do this during the dormant season to help plants grow well in spring and remove any sick or damaged branches. Use clean, sharp tools to make clean cuts that heal quickly and prevent disease. Watch for signs of pests or diseases, like discolored leaves or slow growth, and address them early to avoid serious damage.

Adding trees and shrubs to your dry climate garden helps create a rich and beautiful space that offers shade and homes for wildlife. When picking trees and shrubs, think about their ability to handle dry conditions and how they will fit with the rest of your garden. By choosing the right types and caring for them well, you can make a strong and beautiful garden that benefits the environment and brings you joy.

3.6 Iconic Palm Trees

Palm trees are an iconic part of the California landscape, often seen against the backdrop of the state's beautiful sunsets. From towering, elegant palms to shorter varieties, they are everywhere in California, from homes and streets to the coast. But there's more to palm trees in California than just their beauty.

There are around 20 different kinds of palm trees in California, and they vary in size from small trees, just 3 feet tall, to towering palms that can reach up to 100 feet. Palm trees are in every corner of the state. It's hard to imagine California's cities and coastal towns without them.

Palm trees also have a special meaning. In movies and popular culture, they often represent elegance, comfort, showing you're near a desert oasis or a warm, relaxing place. For travelers, seeing palm trees means they've reached sunny California. Whether standing by a fancy desert hotel or gently swaying by the ocean, palm trees symbolize California's outdoor lifestyle.

If you have a palm tree in your yard, appreciate it. If you're considering adding one to your garden, there are some important things to consider, especially if you live in a dry area.

Native vs. Non-Native Palm Trees

Even though palm trees are a big part of California's identity, only one species is actually native to the state—the **California Fan Palm (Washingtonia filifera)**. This is the only type of palm tree that naturally grows in the western United States. You'll find it in the Colorado and Mojave Deserts and parts of the Coachella Valley. These trees are tough, easy to care for, and can live up to 250 years.

The California Fan Palm

The native **California Fan Palm** is one of the most eye-catching palm trees. It grows to a height of 49 to 66 feet and has large fronds that can spread 20 to 30 feet wide. Each frond can grow up to 13 feet long, creating a large, fan-like canopy at the top of the tree. The trunk is thick and solid, with a brown color that turns gray as the tree ages. This tree is beautiful but low-maintenance and long-lived, making it popular for landscaping.

California Fan Palm Tree

All the other palm trees you see in California have been brought in from other parts of the world. Some popular types include:

The Mexican Fan Palm

A tall, slim palm that can grow over 100 feet high. **The Mexican fan palm is one of the most common palm trees you will see in California**. The Mexican fan palm is a tall, single-stemmed, fast-growing palm tree with a slender, columnar trunk crowned with fan-shaped palmate fronds. Other characteristics of the palm are the swollen base at the trunk, massive 10-foot (3 m) sprays of white flowers, and black, pea-sized fruits.

Mexican Fan Palm Tree

These non-native palm trees have adjusted well to California's climate and are now a common sight, even though they didn't originally grow here.

Mexican Fan Palms, with their sky-high fronds and strong cylindrical trunk, draw the eye up to the sky. They embody the tropical, carefree vibe of a vacation getaway, the perfect addition to a backyard designed for entertaining or relaxing.

Mexican Fan Palms are especially tolerant of desert climates and are high drought, warm weather tolerant. They are low maintenance and do well with yearly professional trimming as they grow out of reach.

The Date Palm

Date palms are a staple of Palm Springs, California's visual landscape and agriculture. The trees were introduced to the area in the late 1800s by the USDA, and have since become a prominent feature of the region.

The date palm is easily recognizable by its upward-growing, arching, feather-like fronds and enormous clusters of red fruits. These date-producing palms have slender trunks with a shaggy appearance, fronds measuring 10 to 16 ft. (3 – 5 m) long, creamy-yellow flowers, and clusters of sweet edible fruits.

Here are some things to know about date palms in Palm Springs:

- Date palms are native to the Mediterranean region, but were imported to California from the Middle East and North Africa.
- Date palms need dry, arid conditions to produce fruit, but also need plenty of water at their roots to withstand the heat.
- Date palms can grow to be 80–120 feet tall.
- Date palms have been cultivated for over 5,000 years

Medjool Date Palm Tree

for their sugary fruit and are still commercially grown today.

The Medjool Date Palm is one of the most famous palm trees. It produces fruit two to three times a year and is both beautiful and tasty, making it popular with both date and palm tree lovers. Its canopy can spread about 25 feet, with silvery, blue-green leaves that grow up to 16 feet long and 2 feet wide. The Medjool is the toughest of the date palms and can grow well in places from California to Florida.

History of Palm Trees in California

Palm trees have been part of California's history for a long time. In the 18th century, Spanish missionaries started planting them for decoration around missions. Over time, more people began planting them, and they became more widespread.

In the late 19th century, Southern California became known as a dream destination, and the introduction of palm trees helped create a tropical, paradise-like image. Tourists loved the look of these exotic trees, and they quickly became a symbol of California's sunny, glamorous appeal.

By the early 20th century, the palm tree became a symbol of California's promise of glamor, sunshine, and exotic beauty. In preparation for the 1932 Summer Olympics in Los Angeles, a large-scale beautification project took place with the planting of over 2,500 palms around the county; many of these palms still stand today. This tree-planting initiative also played a major role in addressing unemployment during the Great Depression, providing work for hundreds of laborers.

California vs. Florida: Who Has More Palm Trees?

Even though California is often linked to palm trees, Florida actually has more palm trees. The tropical climate in Florida allows more types of palms to grow, making it the state with the most palm trees in the country.

How Do Palm Trees Withstand Strong Winds?

Palm trees have several adaptations that help them withstand strong winds and stay upright, including:

- Palm trees typically have root systems that grow down rather than out. Usually they remain within two feet of the trunk and venture down 3-4 feet. The roots spread away from the tree's trunk in an effort to absorb as much water and nutrients as possible.
- Palm trees have fibrous, wet trunks that are made up of many small bundles of woody material, similar to the bundles of wires inside a telephone cable. This structure allows the trunk to bend without snapping.
- Palm trees don't have a big profile on top, so the wind cuts through their fronds.
- Some palm species, like the 100-foot-tall Mexican palms, have evolved to handle annual hurricanes.
- Additionally, some palm species naturally lean as part of their growth habit. This is usually gradual and doesn't threaten the tree's health.

Palm trees are a big part of California's scenery and history. While only one type of palm is native to the state, many others have been brought in from around the world and are now a key feature of

California's landscape. These trees symbolize California's sunny, laid-back vibe and continue to shape how people view the state.

3.7 The Role of Grasses in a Dry Garden

Types of Drought-Tolerant Grasses

Grasses, often overlooked in favor of brighter flowers, play an important role in a dry garden's ecosystem. They're not just fillers; they add movement, texture, and color that can change how your landscape looks and functions.

Blue Fescue is a great choice for ground cover or border plants because of its compact shape and striking blue-gray leaves. It's especially good at creating soft edges along pathways or garden borders and blends well with broad-leaved plants and garden features like rocks. **Mexican Feather Grass** has a light, airy texture with its feathery blades that sway in the breeze. This grass can grow up to two feet tall, adding movement and delicacy to any garden setting.

Benefits of Including Grasses

Adding grasses like Blue Fescue and Mexican Feather Grass to your garden helps with more than just saving water. Their roots bind the soil, preventing erosion from wind and rain, which is especially useful in dry climates. These grasses also make your garden look more attractive, creating soft textures and interesting light patterns.

Designing with Grasses

When designing your garden with grasses, think of them as both a background and a highlight. You can group grasses together to create a flowing, textured look or place them among other plants to add movement and contrast. For a modern garden, you might use grasses in one color to focus on their shapes and textures. In bigger spaces, grasses can cover large areas, providing a light, easy-to-maintain texture that's simpler than a traditional lawn.

Maintenance and Care of Grasses

Maintaining grasses is easy, making them perfect for dry climates. Once established, they need very little water, usually just rainfall. During very dry times, a deep watering now and then helps them grow deeper roots and handle drought better. Trim them back in late winter or early spring to remove old growth and encourage new shoots. Regularly check for pests or diseases, but generally, these grasses are tough and need minimal care.

With their simple beauty and low maintenance, grasses show how to garden effectively with your environment, turning challenges into creative and sustainable solutions.

3.8 Care and Maintenance of Drought-Resistant Plants

Understanding Water Needs

Caring for drought-resistant plants involves understanding their specific needs and creating an environment where they can thrive with minimal effort. Start by figuring out how much water your plants need. Unlike other plants, drought-resistant ones do better with a "less is more" approach. This doesn't mean they never need water; watering should be thoughtful and controlled. Overwatering can cause problems like root rot or fungal growth. To avoid this, use a simple soil moisture test: stick your finger about an inch into the soil; if it feels dry, it's time to water. You might also want to use a drip irrigation system to ensure water gets directly to the roots, reducing evaporation and saving water.

Soil Considerations for Optimal Growth

Soil is the foundation of any garden, and in dry climates, it's especially important to prepare and maintain it well. Start by adding organic matter like compost or aged manure to the soil. This improves the soil's structure, helps it retain moisture, and provides essential nutrients. Mulching is also crucial because it conserves moisture and controls soil temperature, keeping roots cool during hot spells and warm when it's cooler. You can use organic mulches like shredded bark or straw, which add nutrients as they decompose, or inorganic mulches like gravel or pebbles, which reflect heat and reduce evaporation.

Pest and Disease Management

To handle pests and diseases in your garden while being kind to the environment, start with prevention. Choose plants that resist diseases and keep them healthy, as strong plants are less likely to get sick. Regularly check for problems like discolored leaves or slow growth and remove any affected parts to stop issues from spreading. For pests, use natural predators like ladybugs or barriers like row covers to protect your plants. If you need to use products, pick organic ones that focus on specific pests without harming helpful insects or the environment.

Seasonal Care Routines

A seasonal care calendar helps keep your garden healthy and looking good all year. In spring, plant new plants and refresh the mulch. In summer, water regularly and check for pests. In the fall, plant new perennials and shrubs, prune plants, and prepare the garden for winter by clearing debris and adding new mulch. In winter, check for frost damage and plan for spring. Following this schedule helps your garden thrive and fits with the changing seasons.

By using these care strategies, you keep your drought-resistant plants healthy and beautiful and make your garden more sustainable. This thoughtful approach to garden maintenance creates a resilient, vibrant, and harmonious landscape with its natural surroundings, providing a peaceful and sustainable oasis in dry climates.

A successful drought-resistant garden means knowing what your plants need and understanding their environment. The tips on watering, managing pests, and seasonal care are part of a bigger approach that helps your garden thrive while respecting nature. Use these principles and techniques to create a beautiful garden that supports sustainable living.

FOUR

Attracting Wildlife and Supporting Biodiversity

 "In nature, nothing exists alone."

Rachel Carson

Think of your garden as a lively place where butterflies, bees, and birds visit. This chapter shows you how to make your garden a haven for these essential creatures, which will also make your garden more beautiful and eco-friendly. Attracting pollinators and supporting local wildlife means creating a healthy environment, not just adding a few flowers. Let's explore how to make your garden an excellent spot for these helpful visitors.

4.1 Designing Pollinator-Friendly Gardens in Dry Climates

Essential Elements of Pollinator Gardens

To attract pollinators to your garden, you need to think beyond just picking flowers. Consider adding a variety of plants that bloom at different times of the year and provide safe places for pollinators to rest. Bees, butterflies, and hummingbirds are crucial for pollinating plants, including fruits and veggies. By creating a welcoming environment for them, you help your garden thrive and support these important species, which are at risk due to habitat loss and environmental changes.

Plant Choices for Maximum Attraction

The first step in creating a pollinator-friendly garden is to include a variety of plant species. This diversity not only adds beauty with different colors and shapes but also offers a range of food resources for different pollinators. Try to include plants that bloom at different times of the year to provide a continuous food supply. For example, spring flowers like **lavender** and **rosemary** attract early pollinators, while **coneflowers** and **sedum** can feed them through the fall.

Coneflower

Sedum - Autumn Joy

When selecting plants, focus on ones that attract pollinators and do well in dry climates. **Sunflowers** are a favorite for bees and birds because of their large, nectar-rich flowers. **Penstemons** have bright, tubular flowers that are especially appealing to hummingbirds. Try to include native plants whenever possible, as they are usually best suited to your local climate.

Sunflower

Layout Design for Pollinators

The layout of your garden is essential for attracting pollinators. Group similar flowers together to make it easy for pollinators to move from one flower to another. Vary the height of plants to create layers, adding visual interest and making it easier for different pollinators to access the blooms they prefer.

Pollinators also need safe places to rest and reproduce. Old tree stumps, open patches of ground, or "**bee hotels**" made from bundles of hollow twigs can provide bee nesting sites. Butterflies often need specific host plants for their larvae. For example, monarch butterflies lay their eggs only on **milkweed** plants, which their caterpillars later feed on.

Bee Hotel

Milkweed

Avoiding Pesticides

Use as few pesticides as possible to keep your garden friendly to pollinators. Chemical pesticides can harm adult pollinators and their larvae. Instead, try natural pest control methods, like attracting predatory insects such as ladybugs and lacewings, which naturally control pests. If you need to use a pesticide, choose a targeted one, like Bt (Bacillus thuringiensis), which affects only specific pests and is safer for beneficial insects.

4.2 Best Plants for Attracting Beneficial Insects

Benefits of Beneficial Insects

Attracting beneficial insects to your garden succeeds in more than adding beauty; it's a natural way to control pests. Insects like **ladybugs**, **lacewings**, and predatory **wasps** are crucial in maintaining your garden's health by controlling pest populations. Think of these beneficial insects as your garden's natural defense team, patrolling the leaves and soil for harmful pests and stopping infestations before they start. This reduces the need for chemical pesticides, which can harm more than just pests, and creates a healthier environment for your plants to thrive.

Selecting the Right Plants

When selecting plants that attract these beneficial guardians, your focus should be on varieties that offer nectar and pollen or serve as host plants for their larvae. Plants such as **alyssum**, with their tiny flowers, provide an excellent source of nectar for adult insects, while the bright umbels of **fennel** or **dill** are irresistible to many types of beneficial larvae. Herbs like **coriander** and **parsley** add flavor to your dishes and attract lacewings and ladybugs in droves when allowed to flower. Including a range of these plants in your garden ensures that beneficial insects can access the resources they need to survive and help keep your garden healthy.

Companion Planting Strategies

You can integrate these plants into your garden through companion planting, which involves placing plants that benefit each other close together. For example, planting **marigolds** among your tomatoes adds color and attracts beneficial insects that control pests like nematodes. Similarly, planting herbs like **basil** near your vegetables can attract predatory insects that keep pests away while also improving the growth and flavor of your vegetables. The goal is to balance the look and function of your garden, making it a healthy ecosystem.

Creating a Year-Round Habitat

To keep beneficial insects in your garden all year, it's essential to give them food and shelter during every season. In winter, leave some plant debris and fallen leaves to help insects like ladybugs stay warm and protected. Planting evergreen shrubs or grasses also provides shelter in colder months. By designing your garden with these insects in mind, you'll create a space that's beautiful, productive, and easier to maintain, reducing your workload and boosting your enjoyment.

4.3 Water Features for Wildlife in Arid Gardens

Importance of Water in Wildlife Gardens

In a desert garden, a water feature is more than just decorative; it's essential for local wildlife. In dry areas where natural water is scarce, adding a water source provides a lifeline for birds, insects, and other creatures. This simple addition can turn your garden into a thriving, lively ecosystem.

Designing Water Features

As you consider adding a water feature to your garden, consider the options that can be adapted to arid conditions. Simple **birdbaths or shallow dishes** are an excellent start, providing small but vital water sources for birds and insects without requiring extensive maintenance or resources.

For a more permanent fixture, consider a **small pond** or a **recirculating waterfall**. These water features add a visual and auditory element to the garden and support a wider variety of wildlife. These more substantial water features can become focal points in the landscape, drawing the eye while doubling as functional habitats for wildlife. If you choose to design a water feature yourself, it's essential to use materials and plants that reflect the native environment, creating a natural oasis.

Safe and Accessible Designs

When designing water features for a wildlife-friendly garden, safety and accessibility are key. Use shallow edges or sloped sides so small animals and insects can reach the water safely. Adding stepping stones or a gentle slope helps them get in and out easily. Flat rocks or logs partially in the water provide resting spots for birds and insects like bees. These features make the water safer and encourage more wildlife to visit, turning your garden into a busy, lively spot for animals.

Maintaining Water Features

Maintaining water features is essential to keep them clean and safe for wildlife. Regularly remove algae and debris to prevent clogs and maintain water quality. Use natural cleaning methods instead of harsh chemicals to protect animals. If you have a pump, check it often to ensure it works and that water flows well. In colder months, use a small heater or circulator to stop the water from freezing so wildlife can access it all year.

Adding a water feature to your desert garden does more than improve its look—it helps support local wildlife by providing a vital resource. As you enjoy the soothing sound of water and watch animals come and go, you'll see how your garden plays an important role in the environment. This oasis adds beauty, sustains life, boosts biodiversity, and offers a safe space for wildlife in a dry, urban setting.

4.4 Shelter and Nesting: Supporting Fauna Diversity

Types of Shelter

Creating shelters in your garden gives wildlife a safe place to live and helps keep the environment balanced. Every animal that finds a home in your garden adds to its beauty and health. You can design different shelters for various species, ensuring they meet their needs while still looking good in your garden.

Designing for Specific Wildlife

A brush pile is one of the easiest shelters you can make in your garden. Stack branches, leaves, and deadwood in a corner. This gives small animals and birds a safe spot from predators and bad weather. If you can't do this, leave part of your garden a bit wild with rocks, logs, or untouched soil. These areas are essential for ground-nesting bees and other helpful insects, giving them space to live and grow.

Placement of Shelters

For those looking to attract a broader range of birds, installing man-made nesting boxes is a fantastic option. These can be tailored to the birds you wish to attract. For example, bluebird boxes typically have small entrance holes to prevent larger birds from entering, while owl boxes are larger and often placed higher. Placement is key—nesting boxes should be positioned to face away from prevailing winds and with some degree of protection from direct sunlight to avoid overheating. Also, for the birds' safety, ensure they are out of reach from common predators, such as cats and raccoons.

Using Natural and Recycled Materials

Using natural and recycled materials to build shelters benefits wildlife and fits with the eco-friendly approach of a sustainable garden. Old wood, bamboo, and even repurposed items like unused flowerpots can be turned into creative and environmentally friendly shelters. These materials blend well with the garden and ensure your wildlife shelters are as green as the garden.

Creating wildlife shelters in your garden, especially in dry climates, turns it into a sanctuary for various species. Each creature, from pollinating butterflies to singing birds, contributes to the garden's health and beauty. Simple additions like brush piles or nesting boxes support a thriving ecosystem, enhancing your garden and the local environment by promoting biodiversity.

4.5 Seasonal Considerations for Wildlife Support

Understanding Seasonal Needs

Caring for your garden through the seasons also includes supporting the wildlife that visits your space. Each season brings different needs for these creatures, and understanding these needs is crucial for creating a garden that supports a vibrant ecosystem all year. From spring's new growth to winter's quiet dormancy, your garden can be a haven for wildlife if you adjust your efforts to match the seasonal changes.

Spring and Summer Care

Spring and summer are busy times in the garden as many species come out of winter dormancy or migrate back to favorable climates. This period is important for breeding and feeding, offering you a chance to support these processes. You can help by providing protein-rich foods that cater to young wildlife and breeding adults. For birds, set up feeders with sunflower seeds or suet to provide the calories needed for nesting and raising chicks. For insects like butterflies and bees, plant early blooming flowers such as crocuses and daffodils to offer vital nectar sources when not much else is blooming. Maintaining features like mud patches or bare, sandy soil can be crucial for certain bee species that use mud to build nests. These simple additions to your garden not only support the life cycle of these creatures but also improve pollination and the overall health of your garden during the growing season.

Autumn and Winter Strategies

As the vibrant growth of spring and summer fades into the quieter tones of autumn, your garden's focus shifts from growing to getting ready for the colder months. During this season, it's important to make sure wildlife has enough resources to build up energy reserves for winter. Supplemental feeding becomes crucial as natural food sources dwindle. Setting up bird feeders with seeds and nuts can provide essential energy for migrating birds. Instead of deadheading your perennials in autumn, let them go to seed to provide food for birds and small mammals. It's also helpful to leave leaf litter undisturbed in some areas of your garden. This provides insulation and shelter for overwintering insects and enriches the soil as it decomposes.

Winter in the garden is a quiet time, but it still has some needs. Making sure wildlife has access to liquid water can be a lifesaver when natural sources freeze over. Setting up a heated birdbath or using a small pond heater can keep water available. Also, keep putting food in feeders, as many birds depend on these resources in areas where winters are harsh and food is scarce. Providing shelter is also important. Dense evergreen shrubs or piles of brushwood can offer cozy hideaways from the cold, ensuring that your garden remains a refuge against the harsh winter elements.

Year-Round Plant Choices

Plants that provide resources across different seasons are invaluable in creating a garden that supports wildlife year-round. Consider species like holly with its winter berries, lavender for summer nectar, and ornamental grasses that stand tall in the winter, providing shelter and seeds. These plants not only sustain garden visitors throughout the year but also add to the aesthetic and biodiversity of your garden, making it a vibrant ecosystem in every season.

As this chapter wraps up, it's clear that supporting wildlife in your garden is a year-round commitment that brings with it a host of benefits. From the joy of watching a garden teeming with life to the satisfaction of knowing you're contributing to the health of your local ecosystem, the efforts you make in each season can have profound effects. As we move forward, let these insights inspire you to create a garden that not only grows but thrives with life, no matter the season.

4.6 *SPECIAL SECTION!* Desert Wildlife Guests

Wildlife can appear even in planned community settings where you least expect it. Along with pollinators like birds, bees, and butterflies, desert gardens may attract visits from many other creatures. You might encounter raccoons, opossums, squirrels, skunks, rabbits, ducks, and geese. (Yes, really!) And even better than these, you might see Burrowing owls, Fringe-toed lizards,

Desert cottontails, roadrunners, Gamble's quails, Western Diamondback rattlesnakes, the Desert tortoise, and even Desert Bighorn sheep.

The desert is home to over **150 species of animals**. The following are **just a few** of the interesting visitors you may encounter in or near your desert garden:

Western Burrowing owls are small carnivores that eat reptiles, small birds, insects, and rodents. Unlike other owls, they are not nocturnal. They are most active during the day. The owls nest below ground in burrows. (If you feel you are being watched, you probably are.) Look around. This camouflaged owl is sometimes hard to spot. The human population has reduced the charismatic western burrowing owl's breeding populations by more than 60 percent.

Fringe-toed lizards have scaly back toes to help them escape predators and run on sand without sinking, almost like walking on water. Their size is between 6 to 9 inches. They are insectivores. They eat insects, arthropods, flowers, and plants. These are bigger than the average 4 to 6 inch green garden lizard.

Desert cottontails are herbivores that mainly eat grass, leaves, fruit, twigs, and prickly pear pads. They inhabit abandoned burrows of other animals. Cottontail rabbits are most active at dawn and dusk and on moonlit nights. During the day, they hide in dense brush or burrows to avoid predators and harsh weather. When in danger, cottontails will hop away in a zig-zag pattern to confuse their predators.

Roadrunners can run up to 20 mph! Born to run, the Roadrunner can outrun a human, kill a rattlesnake, and thrive in the harsh landscapes of the Desert Southwest. They are omnivores and eat small reptiles, mammals, insects, arachnids, seeds, fruit, and eggs. Roadrunners reach two feet from sturdy bill to white tail tip. As they run, they hold their lean frames nearly parallel to the ground and rudder with their long tails. They like to nest in mesquite trees and cholla cactus. They are commonly seen in residential areas.

Gamble's quails are omnivorous. Their diet consists of seeds, leaves, berries, and small insects. They stay in family groups called coveys. They are non-migratory and are rarely seen in flight. Quails move by walking and can move surprisingly fast through brush and undergrowth. They nest under heavy vegetation. Mothers and chicks are often seen strolling in residential areas. They are highly sociable birds and enjoy communal activities like dust baths.

Desert tortoises are critically endangered. In the Coachella Valley, many are tracked, so if you spot one, contact Animal Control to have it relocated. These tortoises can live up to 80 years but reproduce slowly. It can take up to 20 years to grow to their full size of

14 inches. Despite their slow pace, they eat plants and can travel long distances to find food. They spend most of their time in burrows they dig themselves, using their strong claws to dig up to 30 feet or more.

Western Diamondback rattlesnakes are among the most notorious snakes in the world, known for their venomous bites and distinctive rattles. Their diet consists of small animals such as rabbits, birds, rats, and lizards. Their habitat includes desert shrubbery and rocks. Chances are, you won't encounter a rattler in your yard, but if you do, **back away slowly from this uninvited guest and call Animal Control!**

Desert Bighorn sheep are large herbivores in the cow and goat family. They graze on grass and plants. They are skilled climbers, using their hooves to navigate rocky mountains. On rare occasions, the closer your home is to the mountains, you may see a few of these sheep slowly wander down residential streets, looking for vegetation. Don't approach them. Stay back and let them wander on through. If necessary, call the Police or Animal Control. Keep your camera ready. These sightings are always newsworthy.

On a personal note: Two Visitors stroll from the community pond and take a shortcut through our yard.

Be aware of and prepared for desert wildlife visitors. Be still. Be quiet. **Look, but don't touch!**

FIVE

Water Management Strategies

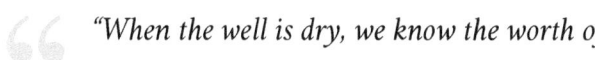

> "When the well is dry, we know the worth of water."
>
> *Benjamin Franklin*

I magine wisely using every drop of water in your garden so that no drop is wasted. Water management is about saving water and making every bit of moisture count in dry climates, keeping your garden lush and vibrant even under the hot sun. This chapter focuses on efficient water use, especially the importance of drip irrigation systems. These systems are not just tools but essential for creating a thriving oasis that can flourish despite the arid conditions around it.

5.1 Drip Irrigation Systems: Setup and Maintenance

Understanding Drip Irrigation

Drip irrigation is perfect for dry climates. It delivers water straight to your plants' roots, where it's needed most. This helps save water and keeps the soil moist, which helps plants grow better. With drip irrigation, water slowly seeps into the soil, encouraging roots to grow deeper and making plants more drought-resistant. It's efficient because it waters only where needed, reducing water waste and minimizing weeds around your plants.

Installation Guide

Setting up a drip irrigation system is easier than it looks if you follow these steps. First, plan where to place the system based on your garden's layout. You'll need a water source, tubing to carry the water, emitters to release it, and maybe a timer to control when it turns on.

1. Attach a backflow preventer to your faucet to protect your water from contamination.
2. Connect a pressure regulator to ensure the water pressure is suitable for your system.
3. Run the main tubing along your garden beds.
4. Cut the tubing and add drip emitters where your plants are.
5. Use tees to branch off the tubing and end caps to close any open ends.

If you want to simplify things even more, add a timer to automate watering. This setup ensures your plants get a steady amount of water, so you don't have to water them manually daily, giving you more time to enjoy your garden.

Maintenance Tips

Keeping your drip irrigation system in good shape helps it work well and last longer. Here's how to maintain it:

1. **Check for Leaks**: Look for leaks in the tubing or connections each month. Leaks can happen if the tubing gets damaged or connections become loose.
2. **Clean the Filters**: Filters can get clogged with debris or minerals, so clean them at least twice during the growing season. You might need to clean them more often if you have hard water.

Regular checks and cleaning will keep your system running smoothly and ensure your plants get the right amount of water.

Another essential maintenance task is flushing your system at the start and end of the growing season. This involves opening the end caps of your drip tubing and running water through the system to flush out dirt or debris. This simple step goes a long way in preventing clogs and ensuring your system delivers water smoothly throughout the season.

Optimization Techniques

Consider using tools like pressure regulators, solar timers, and smart controllers to boost your drip irrigation system. Pressure regulators keep water pressure steady so your garden gets even coverage. Solar timers use energy from the sun, reducing your need for electricity and reducing your carbon footprint.

Smart controllers are advanced irrigation tools that adjust watering based on current weather, soil moisture, and plant needs. They ensure your garden gets the right amount of water, saving resources and keeping your plants healthy.

Setting up a drip irrigation system ensures your garden not only survives but thrives. With thoughtful planning, regular maintenance, and the use of smart technology, you can create a water management plan that's both efficient and effective. This turns the challenge of gardening in a dry climate into a success story of innovation and sustainability.

5.2 Greywater Usage in Gardens: Safety and Efficiency

Defining Greywater

Using greywater, the relatively clean wastewater from showers, dishes, and laundry, is a smart strategy for a sustainable garden, especially in dry climates. Unlike toilet waste, greywater is safe for reuse and helps conserve city water while keeping your garden healthy, even during droughts. Recycling greywater can save 50-80 gallons of water per person daily.

Knowing the source of greywater is essential to using it effectively. Water from showers, bathroom sinks, and washing machines is usually safe for the garden. Avoid water from washing diapers or using harsh chemicals, as these can harm plants. Choose biodegradable, phosphate-free soaps and detergents to prevent soil damage.

Safety Protocols

Safety is crucial when setting up a greywater system. Ensure your system follows local laws and regulations, which can vary widely. Consult with local authorities if you plan to install the system yourself. However, hiring a professional to install greywater systems is recommended. Design it for subsurface irrigation, which keeps greywater below the surface, reducing exposure and preventing pathogen growth.

Safety Design and Implementation

A greywater system uses pipes to divert water from sources like a washing machine to your garden. Your greywater professional will start by installing a diverter valve to choose between sending water to the sewer or garden. The water will be filtered to remove particles and then directed through a buried drain system that delivers moisture to plant roots, reducing waste and runoff.

Efficiency Maximization

Consider adding mulch basins around your plants to improve your greywater system. Basins are small, mulch-filled depressions surrounding your plants' base. They filter out particles, retain moisture, and enrich the soil as the mulch decomposes. They help your plants make the most of every drop of recycled water.

Incorporating a greywater system helps conserve water and keeps your garden thriving in dry climates. Reusing water reduces waste, supports plant health, and creates a more sustainable garden ecosystem.

5.3 Rainwater Harvesting Techniques for Gardeners

Benefits of Rainwater Harvesting

Rainwater harvesting is beneficial in dry climates where saving water is essential. This ancient technique has gained new importance in today's environmentally aware world. It allows you to collect, store, and use rainwater, reducing your need for municipal water systems, which is vital during droughts. Rainwater is soft and free from the salts, minerals, and chemicals found in tap or groundwater, which can help your plants grow healthier and lower soil salinity over time.

Collecting and Storing Rainwater

One of the simplest methods of collecting and storing rainwater is by using rain barrels connected to your downspouts. Water from your roof flows into the barrels when it rains. For larger systems, cisterns are a great option. They can store more water and can be placed above or below ground. Cisterns often have filters to remove debris and bugs and can provide enough water for your garden during dry months.

Integration with Irrigation Systems

You may need to adjust your irrigation system to use collected rainwater in your garden. This could include adding pumps to move water from your storage barrels or cistern to your plants. A small pump can help distribute the water if gravity isn't enough. You might also consider connecting a drip irrigation system to your rainwater storage, delivering water directly to the roots, conserving water, and reducing waste.

Maintenance and Care

Keeping your rainwater harvesting system clean and working well is essential. Regularly check and clean your gutters, downspouts, and screens to avoid blockages. Also, inspect your storage containers for leaks or algae growth, which can happen if tanks are not sealed properly and are exposed to sunlight. To prevent this, use opaque tanks with tight lids. Clean the tanks regularly to remove sediment or debris, ensuring the stored water stays fresh.

By implementing these rainwater harvesting strategies, you make efficient use of a precious resource and contribute to a sustainable gardening practice that enhances the growth of your plants and the beauty of your garden. Integrating rainwater systems demonstrates a commitment to gardening and respecting and preserving the natural environment.

5.4 Scheduling Irrigation: Best Practices for Efficiency

Understanding Plant Water Needs

Managing the watering needs of different plants can be tricky, especially in dry climates where water is limited. Each plant has unique water requirements for where it grows and its root system. For instance, deep-rooted plants like trees and shrubs need less frequent but deeper watering to encourage roots to seek moisture in the soil. On the other hand, vegetables and annuals, which have shallower roots, require more frequent watering in smaller amounts. By adjusting your watering methods to match these needs, you can significantly improve the health and productivity of your plants.

Seasonal weather variations also affect water needs. During the summer, when evaporation rates are high, plants may require more water to cope with the heat. In the cooler months, plants typically grow slower and need less water. By monitoring these seasonal changes and adjusting your watering schedule accordingly, you can avoid underwatering during hot spells and overwatering in cooler weather, which can lead to root rot or fungal diseases.

Creating a Watering Schedule

Creating an efficient watering schedule that meets your garden's needs while minimizing waste is essential. The best times to water are early morning or late evening when it's cooler, and the sun isn't as intense. This helps reduce evaporation and allows water to reach deeper into the soil for plant roots. When planning your schedule, group plants with similar water needs together. This way, you ensure each plant gets the right amount of water and save time and effort on watering.

A weekly watering schedule can help you organize your gardening tasks more efficiently. For example, water your lawn and perennial beds twice a week, while container plants and vegetables might need watering every other day. However, this schedule should not be rigid; it's important to remain flexible and adjust based on current weather conditions. If it rains, you can skip the next scheduled watering, or if a heatwave is forecast, you might need to water more frequently.

Use of Technology

Using technology in your gardening can significantly improve how you manage water. Smart irrigation controllers are excellent tools for this. They automate your watering schedule based on weather, soil moisture, and plants' needs. With sensors linked to local weather data, smart controllers adjust how often and how much you water, considering rainfall, humidity, and temperature changes. This keeps your plants well-watered while preventing water waste, making gardening more sustainable.

Setting up a smart irrigation controller typically involves connecting the device to your home Wi-Fi network and configuring it via a smartphone app. You can input details about your garden, such as plant types, soil conditions, and typical weather patterns, allowing the controller to tailor the watering schedule precisely. Many smart controllers also provide detailed reports on water usage, helping you track your consumption and make further adjustments to improve efficiency.

Adjusting Schedules

Adjusting your watering schedule based on changing conditions is essential for effective gardening. Regularly checking soil moisture helps you see how well your current watering plan works and if you need to make changes. Simple tools like a soil moisture probe can measure moisture at different depths. This information can guide you on whether to water more or less often.

Additionally, observing plant health can also guide your watering decisions. Signs of overwatering include yellowing leaves and a lack of new growth, while underwatered plants may show dry, brittle leaves and stunted growth. Adjust your watering schedule based on these cues to ensure optimal plant health.

By understanding your plants' needs, creating a good watering schedule, using technology wisely, and being flexible with your methods, you can create a lush and efficient garden. This careful approach ensures that every drop of water helps your plants thrive. As you refine your watering practices, each small change will help you find the right balance between conservation and care, which is essential for successful gardening in dry climates.

5.5 Moisture Monitoring and Adjustment Strategies

Importance of Moisture Monitoring

Keeping a close eye on soil moisture levels is like ensuring your garden's thirst is quenched—not too little and certainly not too much. Regular soil moisture monitoring is crucial, especially in a dry climate where water is both a precious and potentially scarce resource. This practice helps you avoid the extremes of overwatering and underwatering, which can lead to various plant health issues. Overwatering can suffocate plant roots and lead to fungal diseases, while underwatering can stress plants and reduce their growth and yield. By consistently checking the soil moisture levels, you ensure that your garden receives just the right amount of water, maintaining plant health and conserving water.

Tools for Moisture Monitoring

In today's tech-driven world, various tools can help you monitor soil moisture accurately, ranging from simple manual methods to high-tech solutions. An essential tool is the soil moisture probe, which you can insert into the soil to get an immediate reading of the moisture level. These probes are inexpensive and easy to use, making them accessible to gardeners of all skill levels. Consider investing in sensor systems that link to smartphones for a more advanced approach. These sensors can provide real-time soil moisture data, which you can access conveniently through an app. This technology allows you to monitor your garden's moisture levels from anywhere, ensuring you're always informed about your garden's needs.

Interpreting Moisture Levels

Interpreting the data from these moisture monitoring tools is vital to making informed irrigation decisions. Understanding what the moisture levels indicate about your garden's water needs helps you adjust your watering schedule effectively. If the moisture sensors show that the soil is consistently wetter than necessary, it may be time to reduce the frequency or duration of your watering sessions. Conversely, if the sensors indicate dry soil, increasing your watering can help bring moisture levels up to an optimal range for plant health. This targeted approach ensures your plants are healthier and conserves water by preventing waste.

To further aid in understanding soil moisture levels, here is a simple chart that categorizes soil moisture readings from dry to wet, helping you decide when to water:

1. Dry (0-10% moisture): Water immediately.
2. Moderate (10-20% moisture): Monitor closely; likely need water soon.
3. Ideal (20-30% moisture): Optimal for most plants.
4. Wet (30%+ moisture): Do not water; allow to dry out to prevent overwatering.

This chart serves as a quick reference to help you interpret moisture data effectively, ensuring your garden receives the right amount of water at the right time.

Using moisture monitoring and adjustment strategies, you can wisely manage your garden's water use. This leads to healthier plants and better yields while helping to conserve water, especially in dry climates. As you better understand soil moisture levels, your garden will thrive, reflecting the care you invest in gardening.

In summary, managing water effectively in your garden depends on accurately monitoring and adjusting soil moisture levels. Using the right tools to collect data and that information to guide how you water your plants, you can keep them healthy and use water efficiently. This proactive approach benefits your garden and helps sustain your local environment. Moving forward, these principles and techniques will be the foundation for sustainable gardening practices that respect and enhance the natural balance of your garden ecosystem.

SIX

Eco-Friendly Gardening Practices

> *"What makes the desert beautiful...is that somewhere it hides a well..."*
>
> Antoine de Saint-Exupery, The Little Prince

Simple, mindful practices like organic mulching can greatly improve your garden's sustainability. These techniques will keep your plants healthy and help create a space that nurtures both the soil and the spirit. Let's dive into organic mulching, where each layer you add is a step toward a more vibrant and eco-friendly garden.

6.1 Organic Mulching: Types and Techniques for Dry Climates

Benefits of Organic Mulch

Organic mulch is a valuable tool for gardeners, especially in dry climates. It offers two main benefits: it conserves moisture and regulates soil temperature. By covering the soil, organic mulch reduces evaporation, so you can water less often while keeping your plants hydrated. This is vital in areas with limited water. Additionally, mulch is a natural insulator, keeping the soil cooler in hot weather and warmer at night. This temperature control is essential for root development and can help extend the growing season for many plants.

As organic mulch breaks down, it adds important nutrients to the soil, improving its quality and helping beneficial microbes thrive. This boosts water retention and encourages healthier plant growth. Using organic mulch not only maintains your garden but also supports its future growth and health.

Selecting the Right Mulch

Choosing the correct type of organic mulch can significantly impact your garden's health and water efficiency. Each type of mulch offers different benefits and looks, so it's important to choose one that suits your garden's needs and your taste. For example, **straw mulch** is lightweight and easy to spread, making it perfect for vegetable gardens. It breaks down quickly and adds organic matter to the soil, but it must be replaced more often.

Pine needles, another popular choice, are perfect for acid-loving plants as they can slightly acidify the soil as they break down. They also tend to stay in place better than lighter mulches, making them a good choice for sloped areas. **Shredded bark**, on the other hand, decomposes slowly and provides a rich, dark color that enhances the visual appeal of any garden bed. It's ideal for ornamental plants and around trees and shrubs, where it can remain undisturbed for extended periods.

When choosing mulch, consider your garden's conditions and plants' needs. Also, consider how the mulch's texture and color will match your garden's look. The right mulch helps your plants and enhances your garden's design.

Application Techniques

To get the most out of mulch, apply it correctly. First, clear away weeds and debris to help block new weed growth. Spread 2 to 4 inches of mulch around your plants, but leave a few inches of space around stems and tree trunks. This gap prevents moisture buildup, which helps avoid rot and fungal issues.

For areas with existing mulch, fluff it up with a rake before adding a new layer. This aeration helps prevent the mulch from compacting, which can restrict water and airflow to the soil. Consider a slightly thicker layer of mulch in garden paths or heavily trafficked areas to withstand the wear and ensure continued effectiveness.

Maintenance and Replenishment

Caring for your mulch is just as important as applying it. Organic mulch breaks down over time, enriching your soil and needing replacement. Check the mulch depth at the start of each growing season and add more as needed to keep it at the right thickness. This helps protect and insulate your soil while keeping your garden looking fresh.

Also, watch for signs of fungal growth or pest infestations in your mulch. Certain types of organic mulch can harbor mold or pests if not monitored. If you notice any issues, it might be necessary to replace the affected mulch to prevent any harm to your plants.

Using organic mulch makes your garden look good and helps your plants thrive. It conserves water, adds nutrients to the soil, and supports a healthy garden ecosystem. Every small step, like mulching, contributes to more sustainable and mindful gardening practices.

6.2 Natural Pest Control Solutions in Arid Gardens

Pests can be challenging in your desert garden, just like the heat. But with the right strategies, you can control them without harmful chemicals. Learn to spot common pests, use natural solutions, and set up preventive measures to keep your garden healthy and thriving.

Identifying Common Pests

Pests like aphids, spider mites, and whiteflies can thrive in dry climates. Aphids are small and come in green, black, or pink colors. They gather on the undersides of leaves, sucking sap and causing curled, distorted leaves. Spider mites are tiny red or brown insects that create delicate webs, leading to yellow, speckled leaves. Whiteflies are small, white insects that fly around when disturbed and cause damage similar to aphids. Spotting these pests early helps prevent severe damage to your plants.

Natural Remedies and Solutions

Once you've spotted pests, natural remedies are a great eco-friendly solution. Introducing beneficial insects like ladybugs, lacewings, and predatory mites can help control pest populations since they prey on common pests. Neem oil, an organic product from the neem tree, acts as a natural insect repellent and disrupts the pests' life cycle. You can also use physical barriers like floating row covers to protect plants while still letting light and water in, ensuring your plants stay healthy.

Preventive Practices

Prevention is key in gardening. Proper plant spacing improves air circulation, reducing humidity and making it harder for pests like spider mites and whiteflies to thrive. Pest-resistant plant varieties can also help, as they naturally defend against specific pests. Regularly clearing away dead leaves and debris helps keep pests from finding places to breed.

These examples highlight how effective integrated pest management (IPM) practices can be in dry gardens. By understanding pests, using natural remedies, and keeping up with preventive practices, you can protect your garden in a safe way for both the plants and the environment. This approach not only preserves your garden's beauty and productivity but also supports healthy and sustainable gardening practices that you can be proud of.

6.3 Composting in Dry Conditions: A Comprehensive Guide

Basics of Composting

Composting is a great way to enrich your garden by turning kitchen scraps and yard waste into nutrient-rich material. It's important to take extra care with your composting system in dry climates. Composting balances carbon-rich materials, called "browns," with nitrogen-rich materials, known as "greens." Browns include dried leaves, straw, and wood chips, which help aerate the compost pile. Greens include kitchen scraps, grass clippings, and fresh plant matter, which provide moisture and nitrogen—both crucial for successful composting.

Challenges and Solutions in Dry Climates

The interaction between carbon-rich and nitrogen-rich materials and enough moisture and air drives the decomposition process, turning raw materials into compost. In dry climates, achieving this balance can be challenging due to low natural moisture levels. Compost piles in arid regions can dry out quickly, slowing down the microbial activity necessary for decomposition. To address this, you can use covered bins or tumblers to help retain moisture and prevent it from evaporating under the hot sun. Adding moisture-retentive materials like **coir** or **vermiculite** can also help maintain the necessary dampness. Regularly turning the compost ensures it gets enough air to support the bacteria that break down the waste while also spreading moisture evenly throughout the pile.

Types of Composting Systems

For dry climates, tumbler bins are especially effective for composting. These bins are sealed and elevated, which helps retain moisture and makes them easy to rotate for consistent aeration. **Vermiculture**, which uses worms to speed up the composting process, is another great option. Worm bins are generally compact and can be kept indoors or in shaded areas to prevent overheating, which is helpful in hot, dry climates. **Pit composting**, where organic matter is buried in shallow pits, can also work well in dry conditions. Covering the pits with thick soil or mulch helps minimize moisture loss.

Benefits to the Garden

Maintaining a compost system in dry gardens offers many benefits. Compost enriches the soil, improves its structure, and helps it retain moisture, vital in arid areas. This better soil structure promotes root growth, allowing plants to access nutrients and water more efficiently. Using compost also reduces the need for synthetic fertilizers, which can harm the environment. Additionally, compost is full of microorganisms that support a healthy soil ecosystem. Over time, regular compost use can transform poor, dry soil into fertile, productive ground, showing that even dry conditions can support thriving gardens.

When you start composting, remember that adjusting for the dry climate will improve your compost and make your gardening more sustainable. Your compost can thrive by selecting the right system and balancing materials, moisture, and air. This will provide a steady supply of nutrient-rich material to boost the health and beauty of your desert garden.

6.4 Creating and Sustaining Biodiversity with Native Plants

Advantages of Native Plant Diversity

Biodiversity in your garden can be considered a colorful mix of native plants, each contributing to the overall health and beauty of your ecosystem. Using a variety of native plants offers several benefits: they are adapted to local conditions, so they require less water and fewer pesticides. These plants have developed alongside local wildlife, creating a supportive environment. They are often more resistant to local pests and diseases, reducing the need for chemicals. Plus, they provide food and shelter for wildlife like birds, butterflies, and beneficial insects, helping to maintain balance in your garden.

Designing for Diversity

Adding a variety of native plants to your garden is a great way to promote sustainability and attract local wildlife. When planning your garden, consider different layers, from tall trees to low ground cover. Each layer should feature plants that thrive in your climate and support various wildlife. For instance, tall native trees provide nesting spots for birds, while lower shrubs offer shelter for small mammals and insects. Ground cover plants like ferns or grasses can attract ground-nesting bees and other beneficial insects. Additionally, including flowering plants that bloom in different seasons ensures a steady food supply for pollinators, keeping your garden lively year-round.

Sustaining Biodiversity

To keep biodiversity in your garden, use practices that support ecological balance. One effective method is rotational planting, where you change the types of plants in specific areas each year. This prevents soil depletion and reduces pests and diseases that thrive on single crops. Adding features like logs, rock piles, or water sources can also help by providing resources and habitats for wildlife. It's important to avoid chemical pesticides and herbicides, as they can harm beneficial organisms. Instead, opt for organic or natural pest control methods to maintain a healthy garden ecosystem.

Embracing biodiversity by using native plants creates a thriving ecosystem that supports all kinds of life. When choosing plants and designing your garden, imagine it as putting together a natural display that highlights the beauty and strength of your local environment. This approach enhances your garden and helps conserve local plants and animals, making your garden an important part of ecological conservation efforts.

6.5 Permaculture Techniques for the Desert Garden

Principles of Permaculture

Permaculture is a way of gardening that works harmoniously with nature, making it an excellent choice for sustainability, especially in dry areas. It's not just a gardening method; it's a philosophy focused on caring for the earth, caring for people, and sharing resources fairly. These central ideas help guide gardening practices that can support themselves and benefit the environment. Permaculture is especially useful in dry climates, as it turns challenges like limited water into chances for creative and sustainable solutions.

Permaculture is an agricultural design approach where the gardener cooperates with the environment. The 12 Principles of Permaculture can be applied to any type of design but generally refer to "permanent agriculture" focusing on perennials rather than annuals. The 12 Principles are the following:

1. Observe and interact
2. Catch and store energy
3. Obtain a yield
4. Apply self-regulation and accept feedback
5. Use renewable resources
6. Produce no waste
7. Design from patterns to details
8. Integrate rather than segregate

9. Use small and slow solutions
10. Use and value diversity
11. Use the edges
12. Creatively use and respond to change

Permaculture principles encourage a connected approach to gardening, where every part has multiple roles and supports each other. In a desert garden, this starts with observing the existing ecosystem. Understanding natural resources like sunlight patterns and how water flows in your area is important. By designing your garden to work with these features instead of against them, you can manage water better, use less energy, and create a garden that fits well into its environment.

Design Elements in Permaculture

In permaculture, design elements like zoning, layering, and using perennial plants help create self-sustaining gardens.

- **Zoning** means organizing your garden into different areas based on how often you use them and how much care the plants need. For example, keep vegetable gardens, which need regular attention, close to your home, while fruit trees, which require less frequent care, can be placed further away.
- **Layering** involves planting different vegetation types at various heights, from ground covers to tall trees. This mimics natural ecosystems and best uses space, light, and nutrients.
- **Perennial plants** live for several seasons and are key to a permaculture garden. They provide stability and ongoing resources for your garden over time.

Water-Wise Permaculture Practices

Water management is crucial to permaculture, especially in dry climates where every drop is essential. Techniques like **contouring** and **swales** can make a big difference. Contouring involves shaping the land to slow down and capture runoff. At the same time, swales, shallow trenches dug along the land's contour, hold water until it soaks into the ground, replenishing groundwater and hydrating the soil. **Keyhole gardens** are another permaculture technique. They are raised beds designed in a circular pattern with a composting basket in the center. This design reduces the space needed for paths and allows efficient watering and nutrient recycling directly from the compost to the plants.

As you think about adding permaculture techniques to your garden, consider it a way of working with nature. This method creates a sustainable and productive garden and respects and improves the ecosystem it is part of. Whether shaping the land to capture rainwater more effectively or planting a food forest that mirrors the natural local landscape, each step in permaculture is about building a future where our gardens and environments can thrive sustainably.

6.6 Eco-friendly Fertilizers and Amendments for Healthy Soil

Types of Eco-friendly Fertilizers

Fertilizers and soil amendments are important to creating a healthy garden, especially in dry climates with limited nutrients and water. To care for your garden without harming the environment, choose eco-friendly options. These natural fertilizers nourish your plants and improve the soil sustainably. Let's look at some natural fertilizers and ways to boost your garden's health while minimizing environmental impact.

Natural fertilizers like **fish emulsion**, **compost tea**, and **green manure** provide a way to feed your plants without using chemicals. Fish emulsion, a byproduct of the fishing industry, is rich in nitrogen, which helps plants grow lush and green. It's easy to apply and quickly absorbed as a liquid, making it great for giving your plants a quick nutrient boost. Compost tea is made by soaking compost in water, creating a gentle, nutrient-rich solution that boosts the microbial life in the soil, helping make nutrients more available to plants. Green manure involves planting crops like clover or alfalfa, then chopping and turning them into the soil to enrich it with organic matter and nutrients as they decompose. These methods nourish plants and improve the soil's ability to hold water and nutrients.

Soil Amendment Techniques

To improve your soil, adding organic matter is essential. Materials like compost, leaf mold, and well-rotted manure help the soil hold moisture and nutrients better. **Biochar**, a type of charcoal, is especially useful in dry climates because it retains water and nutrients near the roots, reducing how often you need to water. **Mycorrhizal fungi** are another great addition; they work with plant roots to help them absorb more water and nutrients. Using these amendments can turn even tough soils into rich environments for your plants.

Application Guidelines

Using these fertilizers and amendments correctly takes some knowledge. For liquid fertilizers like fish emulsion and compost tea, apply them directly to the soil around the plants or use them as a spray for quick absorption. It's best to do this during the cooler parts of the day to prevent evaporation and ensure efficient nutrient absorption. For soil amendments like biochar and compost, work them into the top few inches of soil or apply them as a top dressing. Timing is essential; early spring or fall is ideal because it gives the soil time to incorporate the amendments before the planting season. Remember, moderation is key; too much fertilizer can cause nutrient runoff, polluting nearby waterways.

Environmental Benefits

The environmental benefits of using eco-friendly products are significant. Avoiding synthetic fertilizers reduces the risk of chemical runoff, which can contaminate water sources and harm local wildlife. Natural fertilizers and amendments improve soil health by boosting biodiversity and resilience to pests and diseases. This reduces the garden's carbon footprint and helps create a healthier, more sustainable ecosystem.

Integrating eco-friendly practices into your gardening routine contributes to a larger movement toward sustainability. Each time you choose natural fertilizers and amendments, you take a step toward nurturing your garden in a way that respects and preserves the environment.

SEVEN

Solving Common Problems and Challenges

 "You can't fight the desert. You have to ride with it."

Louis L'Amour

Stepping into your garden under the relentless desert sun can feel like walking into a hot oven. However, with the right strategies, you can transform your sun-drenched space into a resilient paradise that thrives even in the hottest summer heat. This chapter explores managing extreme heat and sun exposure challenges in a dry climate garden. By understanding plant heat tolerance, using smart sun protection strategies, making wise irrigation adjustments, and using innovative materials like reflective mulches, you'll learn how your garden can survive and thrive under the sun's intense gaze.

7.1 Managing Extreme Heat and Sun Exposure

Understanding Plant Heat Tolerance

The ability of plants to survive in extreme heat is a fascinating blend of biology and environment. Plant heat tolerance is more than the ability to survive the scorching sun; it's about how they adapt internally to keep functioning. Some plants are naturally suited to hot climates, while others are bred to handle heat. When selecting plants for your garden, look for those with proven heat tolerance. These plants often have deeper root systems that reach cooler soil layers or leaves with reflective surfaces that minimize water loss. **Succulents**, with thick, moisture-retentive leaves, and small-leafed shrubs like **Rosemary** and **Lavender**, which reflect solar radiation, are great options. Also, local plants are usually adapted to handle your area's heat better.

Sun Protection Strategies

Creating shade in a desert garden requires careful planning, choosing the right plants, and using shade structures. For delicate plants, you can use **shade cloths** to block some sunlight, making the area cooler. This protects young plants or vegetable gardens during the hot summer. You can also plant **tall, leafy trees or shrubs** to provide natural shade for smaller plants, reducing heat. Another option is using **plant sunscreens**, sprays applied to reduce **transpiration** and protect against UV damage. These can be very helpful during heatwaves or hot days.

Transpiration

Transpiration is similar to evaporation. It's the process where plants lose water from their leaves, like how animals and humans sweat to cool down.

Irrigation Adjustments for Heat Waves

When the heat rises, keeping your garden hydrated becomes more challenging. Traditional watering methods often aren't enough as evaporation rates increase. During heatwaves, **adjust your watering schedule** to early mornings or late evenings when it's cooler so water can soak deeply into the soil without much loss to evaporation. You might need to water more often, but be careful not to overwater, which can cause root rot or fungal diseases. **Drip irrigation systems**, which deliver water directly to the roots, can be especially effective in ensuring water is used efficiently and plants stay healthy.

Reflective Mulches

Reflective mulches are like having a secret weapon for your garden. These innovative materials reflect sunlight away from the soil, lowering the soil temperature and helping keep plant roots cool. You can use materials like **plastic silver mulch** or organic options like **straw sprayed with reflective white paint**. These mulches keep pests away and make water use more efficient by reducing evaporation. Placing reflective mulch around plants sensitive to heat creates a cooler environment that protects them from the intense sun, helping them thrive despite the heat.

Using these strategies in your garden, helps your plants survive and thrive as temperatures rise. These methods go beyond just dealing with the heat; they help create a garden that is strong, resilient, and full of life, turning challenges into successes. As you make changes, try new things, and watch your garden grow, it becomes a beautiful space reflecting your adaptability and care.

7.2 Overcoming Poor Soil Conditions: Tips and Tricks

Building a successful garden in dry climates begins with the soil. It's more than just a foundation; it's a living ecosystem that plays a significant role in your garden's health. You can transform your garden into a thriving space by understanding and fixing common soil issues like low organic matter or unbalanced pH. Let's look at identifying these problems and using simple strategies to improve your soil, creating the best environment for your plants.

Identifying Soil Deficiencies

The first step to improving poor soil is understanding its condition. Soil low in organic matter often looks dry, compact, and doesn't hold water well, which is a big issue in dry climates. To check your soil, grab a handful and feel its texture. If it's hard and clumps together, it likely has **too much clay** and drains poorly. If it crumbles and feels gritty, it probably has **too much sand**, meaning it drains quickly but lacks nutrients. For more accurate results, consider a soil test. This will show the soil's nutrient levels and pH, helping you know what to add for improvement. You can find soil test kits at garden stores or send a sample to a local extension service for a detailed analysis.

Enhancing Soil Fertility

After identifying what your soil is lacking, the next step is to enrich it. Adding organic compost is one of the best ways to improve soil fertility. Compost provides essential nutrients and improves soil structure, making it easier for roots to grow and for water to penetrate and be retained. Another great amendment is **worm castings**, rich in nutrients and beneficial microbes that help break down organic matter into forms that plants can absorb. You can also use **green manures**—crops like **clover** or **alfalfa** grown specifically to be plowed back into the soil. These plants add organic matter and fix nitrogen, a crucial nutrient for plant health, boosting soil fertility.

Improving Drainage

If your soil is **compacted or clay-heavy**, improving its drainage is crucial. Poor drainage can lead to waterlogged soil, which deprives roots of oxygen and makes your plants more susceptible to root rot. One effective technique is to **build raised beds**, which elevate the soil above ground level and naturally enhance drainage. If raised beds aren't an option, consider **manually aerating your soil** by turning it over and mixing in coarse sand or organic matter like peat moss, which can help break up dense clay particles and improve water flow. Regularly incorporating organic matter improves drainage over time and enhances soil life, which keeps the soil loose and well-aerated.

Soil pH Adjustments

The pH level of your soil is crucial for how well plants can absorb nutrients. Most plants thrive in slightly acidic to neutral soil, with a pH of 6.0-7.0, but dry-climate soils can sometimes be alkaline. If your soil test shows a high pH, you can lower it by adding **elemental sulfur**, which makes the soil more acidic. On the other hand, if the soil is too acidic, you can raise the pH by applying **garden lime** to bring it closer to neutral. It's important to add these amendments in moderation and follow package directions closely, as large swings in pH can shock plants and disrupt soil biology.

By addressing these common soil issues, you're setting the stage for a garden that's not only beautiful but resilient. Improved soil leads to stronger, healthier plants that can withstand the challenges of a dry climate, from drought to heat waves. So, take the time to understand and nurture your soil—it's a fundamental step in cultivating a garden that will delight and sustain you year after year.

7.3 Dealing with Common Diseases and Pests in Dry Areas

Dealing with the challenges of a dry climate garden involves more than just managing water and sun; pests and diseases can also threaten your hard work. However, you can protect your garden by focusing on prevention, early detection, and sustainable solutions. Let's explore strategies that keep these issues at bay and help create a healthier, more vibrant garden ecosystem.

Preventive Measures

The key to a healthy garden is prevention. Simple strategies like proper plant spacing, choosing disease-resistant varieties, and keeping your garden clean can greatly reduce pests and diseases. Giving plants enough space ensures good air circulation, which helps prevent fungal infections like powdery mildew. It's also important to pick plants that naturally resist diseases common in your area; you can find this info on plant tags or by asking local nurseries or gardening experts. Regularly cleaning up fallen leaves and diseased plant parts prevents the spread of pathogens and removes breeding grounds for pests. By following these practices, you create a garden environment that is less attractive to pests and diseases.

Identifying Common Diseases

Spotting garden diseases early can really help you manage them better. In dry climates, **powdery mildew** and **root rot** are common problems. Powdery mildew looks like white, powdery spots on leaves and stems. It does well in warm, dry areas, especially when there's a lot of humidity at night. Root rot usually happens because of overwatering or poor drainage and shows up as wilted, yellowing leaves and stunted growth. To deal with these issues, keep an eye on your plants regularly for any signs of trouble. If you think a plant is diseased, isolate it to stop the spread and remove any sick parts. You can use a **homemade baking soda spray** (mix a teaspoon of baking soda with a quart of water) to handle mild cases of powdery mildew. You'll need to improve drainage and change your watering habits for root rot to help your plants get back on track.

Eco-Friendly Pest Control

When pests show up in your garden, using eco-friendly solutions can effectively control them without harming your garden's ecosystem like synthetic pesticides can. You can use biological controls, like introducing **beneficial insects such as ladybugs**, to manage pests like aphids naturally and provide long-term pest control. Another option is **homemade organic insecticides**, like **neem oil** or **insecticidal soap**, which target pests but leave beneficial insects alone. These methods should be part of an integrated pest management strategy that includes physical controls like barriers or traps and practices such as crop rotation and choosing pest-resistant plant varieties. By using these environmentally friendly methods, you not only keep your garden healthy but also support the local ecosystem's health.

Monitoring and Early Detection

When managing diseases and pests in your dry climate garden, remember that the goal isn't to create a sterile environment but to build a balanced ecosystem where plants can thrive despite challenges. By incorporating prevention, early detection, and eco-friendly solutions into your gardening routine, you create a garden and a sanctuary that supports a diverse range of life.

7.4 Windbreaks and Other Solutions for Windy Areas

Creating a stable environment is crucial for protecting and nurturing your plants when gardening in windy conditions. Wind can dry out soil, damage plants, and destroy valuable topsoil. However, with some smart planning and design, you can turn this challenge into a garden feature that protects and enhances your space. Designing effective windbreaks and choosing the right plants can make a big difference in helping your garden stand strong against the wind.

Designing Effective Windbreaks

Creating effective windbreaks means understanding how wind moves through your garden. By observing the direction of the wind during different seasons, you can place barriers that slow down the wind without blocking it completely. **Living wind-**

breaks, like hedges or rows of trees, work well because they reduce wind speed without causing turbulence. For example, a hedge of dense evergreens can filter the wind, slowing it down without creating the swirling effects that a solid fence might cause. These living barriers also add biodiversity to your garden by providing habitats for birds and beneficial insects, helping to balance the ecosystem.

Besides using living windbreaks, you can also use **non-living structures like walls or fences**, especially in open areas where you need quick results. Materials like **woven wattle fences** or **trellises** with climbing plants can help block the wind and add a nice decorative touch to your garden. Let some air pass through these structures, which helps diffuse the wind's energy. This way, you avoid creating a solid barrier that could cause the wind to swirl and possibly harm your plants.

Plant Selection for Windy Areas

Choosing the right plants for windy areas is vital in helping them survive and grow. These plants need to be tough enough to handle the physical stress from the wind and adjust to the quick evaporation that wind can cause. **Grasses** are great for windy spots because their flexible stems bend instead of breaking, and their deep roots keep the soil in place, reducing erosion. Tall, sturdy perennials like **Russian Sage** and **Goldenrod** also do well in the wind. Their strong roots keep them anchored, and their hardy stems stand up to the breezes. These plants survive and thrive in windy conditions, adding structure and color to your garden.

Structural Support for Plants

Providing support for taller plants and young trees is critical in windy gardens. **Stakes** and **trellises** can give these plants the extra help they need until they're strong enough to stand independently. When staking a tree, put the stakes on the side facing the wind and use flexible ties so the tree can move a bit. This movement helps the tree develop a stronger root system, making it more stable. For climbers or taller perennials, a trellis or a series of supports can help them grow upright without being knocked over by the wind.

Mitigating Wind Erosion

Preventing wind erosion is crucial for maintaining soil health and stopping topsoil loss. **Ground cover plants** are excellent for protecting the soil; their dense growth shields the soil from the wind, their roots bind the soil particles together, and they help retain moisture. **Mulching** is another effective technique; organic mulches like **wood chips** or **straw** reduce soil erosion by cushioning the soil surface against the wind. Applying a thin layer of heavier mulch like **pebbles** or **shredded rubber** in vulnerable areas can help anchor the soil further, providing extra protection against wind erosion.

Using these strategies in your garden design can protect your plants from the wind, helping your garden thrive even in breezy conditions. These techniques do more than just shield your plants; they also boost your garden's beauty and stability, creating a resilient space that stays strong no matter how hard the wind blows.

7.5 Strategies for Sloped Landscapes and Erosion Control

Gardening on a slope can be challenging and might require professional help for tasks like terracing and building retaining walls. It's important for home gardeners to understand these tasks and how they work. Depending on your skill level, you can often tackle these challenges with DIY solutions. With some planning, you can transform sloped gardens into attractive and productive spaces, reducing erosion and creating easier-to-manage planting areas.

Terracing and Retaining Walls

Terracing means building flat areas on a slope, each held up by a **wall** or **embankment.** This helps stop soil erosion and makes it easier to maintain your garden. Instead of a steep hill, you get level, raised beds for planting. To make sure the terracing works well, it's important to have proper drainage to avoid water pooling and pressure on the lower terraces. Well-built terraces give you more planting space and reduce maintenance work.

Terrace

Retaining walls, which can be made from **stone**, **wood**, or **concrete**, help hold back soil and create flat areas for planting. They need to be strong and securely anchored into the slope to handle the pressure from the soil. It's important to include drainage solutions like **weep holes** or **gravel backfill** to release trapped water and reduce pressure on the wall. Retaining walls are functional and can add beauty to your landscape.

Retaining Wall

Choosing Plants for Slopes

Choosing the right plants for terraced or retained areas is important. **Deep-rooted plants** like **native grasses** or certain **shrubs** help stabilize the soil and prevent erosion. Native grasses like **switchgrass** or **bluestem** have extensive root systems that are great for soil retention. Shrubs like **cotoneaster** or **juniper** also help and add variety to your garden. Planting these at the edges of terraces or behind retaining walls can greatly enhance the stability of your sloped garden.

Water Diversion Techniques

Water diversion techniques like **swales** and **French drains** are great for managing runoff in sloped gardens. **Swales are shallow, grassy channels** that slow down and capture runoff, letting it soak into the ground instead of washing away soil and nutrients. **French drains use a buried perforated pipe** in a gravel-filled trench to capture and redirect excess water. Both methods help prevent erosion and ensure that water reaches your plants without taking the soil with it.

Maintenance Tips

Maintaining a sloped garden requires a few additional considerations, especially for watering and fertilizing. **Water slowly and deeply, using drip irrigation**, if possible, to ensure moisture penetrates the soil and encourages deep root growth. **Use slow-release fertilizers or organic compost** to prevent wash-off. Mulching is also important; it helps retain moisture and prevents soil erosion.

Using these strategies, your sloped garden can become beautiful and sustainable. Building terraces, installing retaining walls, and planting erosion-controlling species solve problems and add value to your garden. If the task seems overwhelming, consider getting professional help to ensure everything is done correctly. With the right approach, even the steepest hill can be tamed and transformed into a thriving, vibrant garden.

7.6 Reviving a Neglected Dry Climate Garden

Stepping into a neglected garden that's been left to fend for itself can feel daunting. Overgrown paths, weeds, and stressed plants can overwhelm a garden. However, with a systematic approach and some gardening elbow grease, you can breathe new life into a neglected garden.

Assessing the Garden's Condition

Start by checking the garden's condition. Walk around and see which plants can be saved and which areas need work. Look for plants that are still alive and spots full of weeds or debris. This quick check helps you focus on the most critical tasks so you don't waste time or resources on areas that can't be fixed.

It's time to get to work and start cleaning up. Begin by removing debris, dead plants, and weeds to stop pests and diseases from spreading. This will also give you a better view of the garden, making it easier to plan your next steps. Be careful with the soil as you clean so you don't disturb dormant seeds or helpful organisms supporting the garden's recovery.

Restoration Plan

Create a step-by-step plan to restore your neglected garden. Focus first on tasks that improve its health and appearance. Start with **soil improvement**, then **fix structures** like fences or trellises. Finally, focus on **plant arrangement and choices** to enhance the garden's look.

Reintroducing native plants is essential for your restoration plan. They thrive better in local conditions, needing less water and nutrients. They also support local wildlife and boost garden biodiversity. Use a mix of ground covers, shrubs, and trees for a layered, attractive, and functional garden.

Revitalizing Soil

Revitalizing soil in a neglected garden is crucial for healthy plant growth. Start by **aerating** with a garden fork or aerator to break up compacted soil, allowing air and water to penetrate deeper. This helps roots grow better and improves soil structure.

Add **compost, manure, or leaf mold** to replenish nutrient-depleted soil. These improve soil texture and moisture retention and support beneficial microbes. Add sand or clay breaker to improve texture and fertility for sandy or clay-heavy soil.

Proper rehydration techniques are also critical, especially in dry climates. Use a **drip irrigation system** to provide consistent, targeted hydration without overwatering. **Mulch with straw or bark** chips to retain soil moisture and reduce temperature fluctuations, creating a stable environment for plant roots.

Long-Term Improvement Strategies

Gradually add drought-tolerant plants that need less water and care for long-term improvement. Research **native plants** with low water needs that fit your soil type and sun exposure.

An efficient irrigation system, such as drip irrigation or soaker hoses, can be used to conserve water by targeting plant roots and reducing evaporation and runoff. Consider a **rainwater harvesting system** to utilize natural rainfall and lessen the need for additional watering.

Establishing regular maintenance routines is the final piece of the puzzle. Regularly **checking plants for signs of stress or disease**, **pruning as needed** to encourage healthy growth, and **adjusting watering schedules** according to the seasons are all practices that will keep your garden vibrant year after year.

Revitalizing a neglected garden can be challenging, but by carefully assessing the space, creating a structured restoration plan, and making targeted interventions, you can turn an unfriendly, neglected space into a flourishing, sustainable garden.

In the next chapter, we'll explore advanced techniques and future trends in dry climate gardening, helping you stay ahead in creating a garden that's not only resilient but also cutting-edge in its approach to sustainability and design.

EIGHT

Advanced Techniques and Future Trends

> "Conservation means development as much as it does protection."
>
> *Theodore Roosevelt*

Modern irrigation technology can now monitor your watering systems to deliver more than just timed irrigation; it can monitor the individual needs of the plants in your garden. As we explore the latest advancements in smart irrigation technology, you'll discover how these cutting-edge systems can transform your gardening routine, making it more efficient and aligned with the rhythms of nature.

8.1 The Emerging Smart Irrigation Systems

Today's smart irrigation systems are a big improvement in gardening technology. They use sensors and advanced algorithms to adjust watering based on real-time data like soil moisture, temperature, and weather forecasts. **Soil moisture sensors** can tell when the soil is dry and turn on the irrigation system to water your plants when needed. These sensors can be especially helpful during unexpected dry spells or heat waves when manual watering is insufficient.

Temperature sensors are also important because they adjust the watering schedule based on the heat. If a heatwave is predicted, the system increases watering to prevent plant stress. **Weather prediction algorithms** in some advanced systems use delay watering if rain is expected, which helps save water and prevents over-saturating the soil. This technology saves water, which is important in dry climates, and keeps your garden looking healthy and vibrant without any extra work from you.

Benefits of Automation

You can now manage your garden's irrigation from your phone, whether you're home or away. Automated smart irrigation systems make this easy and offer great benefits for both the garden and the gardener. They significantly reduce water waste compared to traditional systems, which often use water inefficiently, especially during times when evaporation rates are high. Automated systems use water only when and where needed, saving water and reducing utility bills, giving you more time to enjoy yourself and focus on other gardening tasks.

Integration with Home Automation

Smart irrigation systems are now connected to home automation networks, making things more efficient. It's not just for convenience; these systems work together. For example, your irrigation system can link to your weather station and water supply to adjust water usage based on indoor and outdoor conditions.

You can manage your garden's watering schedule using the same apps you use for your home's lighting, heating, and security systems. With platforms like Google Home or Amazon Alexa, you can control your irrigation system with voice commands, making garden management as easy as talking.

Future Trends in Irrigation

In the future, irrigation technology will become more personalized and adaptive. Artificial Intelligence (AI) is making more innovations in smart gardening, with systems that learn from a lot of data to make accurate predictions about watering needs. An irrigation system could know when to water based on current soil moisture and weather conditions and predict your garden's needs based on past conditions.

These systems might be able to diagnose plant health issues based on changes in watering patterns and alert you to problems before they become visible. As these technologies improve, they promise to make gardening more intuitive and responsive, helping even novice gardeners become more skilled in creating highly sustainable and efficient gardens.

8.2 Advances in Soil Science for Water Conservation

Hydrogels and Super Absorbent Polymers

In gardening, the soil has secrets to saving water, and science is helping us learn them. One big innovation is using **hydrogels** in agriculture. Hydrogels are super absorbent, gel-like materials that can hold a lot of water and release it slowly to plants. They can soak up water during rain or watering and then gradually release it back into the soil during dry times. Hydrogels are especially useful in sandy soils, which usually don't retain water well. Adding hydrogels to the soil can make these fast-draining soils more moisture-rich for your plants.

To use hydrogels, mix them into the soil at the root level during planting. They will absorb and release water as needed. Using hydrogels also helps create a more stable environment for your plants by reducing the risks of overwatering and underwatering, leading to healthier and more resilient gardens.

Soil Sensors and Analysis Technology

Soil science has developed **advanced soil sensors** that provide real-time data on soil health. These sensors act like a continuous soil health checkup, monitoring moisture levels, nutrient content, and soil pH. You can view this information through simple, user-friendly apps on your smartphone or computer. If a nutrient is low, you'll know which supplement to add, ensuring your plants have the best growing conditions. Real-time data collection allows you to make timely adjustments, preventing plant stress or disease and keeping your garden healthy throughout the season.

Developments in Soil Amendments

Significant advancements in soil amendments have been made, especially those that improve water retention and reduce evaporation. **Biochar**, a type of charcoal, is popular because it retains nutrients and moisture in the soil. It is particularly useful in sandy soils where water drains quickly. Another development is **advanced composts** with water-absorbing materials that improve water retention. These new composts help keep the soil moist during hot summers, reducing the need for extra watering and helping your garden thrive.

Impact of Soil Science on Water Conservation

These advancements in soil science significantly impact water conservation. Keeping the soil moist and nutrient-rich with less water is groundbreaking in agriculture and landscaping. It allows crops and gardens to thrive with minimal water, conserving this vital resource. These technologies provide new ways to grow food and maintain green spaces without depleting water supplies in areas with water shortages. By adopting these soil management strategies, you're improving your garden and contributing to a global effort to use land more sustainably and protect our planet's resources.

8.3 Reflecting on the Global Implications of Water-Smart Gardening

Global Water Scarcity Issues

Water is essential for life on our planet and vital for humans and all ecosystems. However, water scarcity is becoming a serious issue due to climate change and population growth. In many areas, water that used to be plentiful is now becoming scarce. Gardening, a popular activity that connects people with nature, can help address water scarcity. Sustainable gardening practices that improve water efficiency are not just helpful; they are essential for the future of our gardens and communities.

Adaptation Strategies for Different Regions

Gardening practices are changing around the world to adapt to new water challenges. In the dry American Southwest, gardeners are choosing native plants that need less water, helping to save resources. In Southeast Asia, where monsoons bring heavy rain, rainwater harvesting systems are becoming popular. These systems collect and store rainwater during the wet season to use during the dry months. This saves municipal water and helps reduce runoff into local rivers and streams.

Adaptation strategies involve not just individual gardeners but also community and city efforts. For example, cities like Singapore have created green spaces with sky gardens and vertical planting systems that use smart irrigation technologies. These systems adjust watering based on current weather conditions, helping to use water more efficiently and reduce waste. This approach demonstrates how urban areas can become green and vibrant without worsening water scarcity.

Educational Impacts

Education is key to adopting water-smart gardening techniques. Raising awareness about sustainable gardening practices is important, especially as water scarcity becomes more serious. Educational programs can teach gardeners how to use water-efficient techniques, select the right plants, and design gardens that conserve water naturally. Local gardening clubs, botanical gardens, and extension services can offer workshops and resources tailored to community needs. By providing gardeners with knowledge and skills, we encourage a culture of sustainability that supports water conservation.

Think about how you can use water-smart gardening in your garden. Whether by installing a new irrigation system, trying drought-resistant plants, or setting up a rainwater harvesting system, each change helps conserve water

Share your garden, share what you have learned, and take pride in your achievements. Your dedication and success have established you as an advocate of water conservation and eco-friendly gardening.

Conclusion

 "Unless someone like you cares a whole awful lot, nothing is going to get better, it's not."

Dr. Seus - The Lorax

This book is here to help you, the Gardener, understand the environmental challenges of desert and dry climate gardening. We began by exploring the unique challenges and opportunities of arid environments and then moved on to techniques that make our gardens both sustainable and vibrant.

Water conservation has been the primary focus. We've investigated new irrigation methods, soil improvements, and smart plant choices that keep our gardens thriving and show what's possible in water-efficient gardening. Every bit of water saved helps our planet.

By using sustainable practices like planting native species and encouraging biodiversity, we're doing more than just gardening. We revisited familiar plants and discovered many more plants that could become the highlight of our desert garden. We learned how to evaluate and treat the desert soil, how to choose and plant trees, shrubs, and flowers that will thrive in and enjoy the arid landscape, how to choose plants and design their placement to support local wildlife habitats, and we have even been introduced to many of the surprising wildlife visitors we may encounter on our gardening journey.

Successful dry climate gardens depend on choosing the right plants, efficient water management, promoting biodiversity, and dealing with the usual challenges of these environments. Moving forward, adopting new trends and staying innovative will keep our gardens thriving.

I hope you have enjoyed this tour of creating a dry-climate garden, which included the meadow garden, the succulent and cacti gardens, the perennial, annual, and rose gardens, the grasses, the pollinator gardens, the trees, the shrubs, and the iconic palm trees. And, of course, the look into the desert wildlife we may share these gardens with.

From my experience, there's nothing like the joy of seeing a garden thrive despite challenges. It's incredibly rewarding to watch a desert marigold bloom, feel the breeze through a Palo Verde tree, and watch the aerial play between the birds, bees, and butterflies!

I encourage you, fellow garden enthusiasts, to apply the tools and insights from this book to your gardens. Each small step you take —a new drought-resistant plant here, a water-saving technique there—contributes to a larger global effort for sustainable living. Even with limited resources, gardens can be full of life and color, showcasing the gardener's effort and creativity.

You are more than a gardener. You are a Steward of the Earth. Be proud of what you are doing. And, yes, enjoy the results!

Happy gardening!

Dian Eaton

Your Chance to Help Others Create Water-Wise Colorful Desert Gardens

By sharing your honest opinion of **THE DESERT GARDEN**, you'll help fellow gardeners find the information they need to create thriving, lush, native plant gardens in dry-climate regions.

Thank you for your support. Your review will have more impact than you might imagine.

Scan the QR code below to leave your review!

About the Author

Dian Eaton is an author of gardening books, young adult, and children's books. This book, ***The Desert Garden: You Can Be Water-Wise and Still Create a Lush, Colorful, Native Plant Oasis***, is the third in a series of sustainable gardening books. The first book in the series is ***The Meadow Garden: Create a Low-Maintenance Wildflower and Native Plant Wonderland***, followed by the second book, ***The Pollinator Garden: How to Attract Nature's Heroes - Planting for Birds, Bees, and Butterflies***. Dian is also a painter, actor, and songwriter. She has a degree in Theater Arts and has performed on stage, in films, and on television. Dian lives with her family in Southern California and pursues her passions: gardening, writing, and painting.

Resources

For more information on drought-tolerant gardening, pollinators, plant and animal conservation programs, and wildlife organizations, here are some wonderful sites to visit:

- The Living Desert Zoo and Botanical Gardens https://livingdesert.org
- The Water Conservation Garden in San Diego, CA www.thegarden.org
- World's Largest Rose Tree ·Rose Tree Museum (tombstonerosetree.com)
- Pollinator Conservation Program https://www.xerces.org/pollinator-conservation
- The Bee Conservancy https://thebeeconservancy.org/
- Lady Bird Wildflower Center www.wildflower.org
- American Horticultural Society www.ahsgardening.org
- National Wildlife Federation https://www.nwf.org/
- San Diego County Water Authority SCDWA.org/conservation, watersmartsd.org
- USDA U.S. Department of Agriculture https://www.usda.gov/
- U.S. Fish and Wildlife Service https://www.fws.gov/
- US Forest Service www.fs.usda.gov/managing-land/wildflowers/pollinators/importance

References

Quotes

Attenborough, David quotes https://www.goodreads.com/quotes/search/david+attenborough

Fairbrother, Nan quotes https://www.goodreads.quotes/search/nan+fairbrother

Carson, Rachel quotes https://www.goodreads.com/search/quotes/rachel+carson

Franklin, Benjamin quotes https://www.goodreads.com/search/quotes/benjamin+franklin

Saint-Exupery, Antoine https://www.brainyquote.com/authors/antoine+saintexuper

L'Amour, Louis https://www.brainyquote.com/authors/louis+L'Amour

Roosevelt, Theodore quotes https://goodreads.com/search/quotes/theodore.roosev

Seuss, Dr. quotes https://www.goodreads.com/search/quotes/Dr.+Seuss

Photos

iStock - 1278682898 - Desert garden
Pexels - 3693409_1280 Succulents
Pexels - 4921883 - Agave
Pexels - 7105718 - Buffalo grass
Pexels - 14425533 - Desert marigold
Pexels - 64227 - Palo verde tree
Pexels - 897692 - Joshua Tree
iStock - 1595584_1280 Lavender
Pexels - 432-786 - Pensteman firebird
iStock - 168616920-2048 - front garden
Pexels - 455209_1280 - ornamental grass
Pixabay - 1073282 _640 - Bird of Paradise
iStock - 13527281280 - Poppy
Pixabay - 021521 - Blue Grama grass
iStock - 172732160-612 x612 Succulents
iStock - 1488273533-612x612 Desert yard
iStock - 1413360092-612x612 - Paver path

References

Pixabay - 458ee9da10c270131xcdea735efe442ebe - Ground cover
Pixabay - 0007772-weihenstephane - Gold sedum
iStock - 217347937-612x612 - Succulents
Pexels - 3460497-640 - Succulents
Pexels - 453386530 - Succulents in fountain
Getty - 0758273d2e734183ae2e7e92dfd96c0 - Succulents on wall
Pexels - soly-moses-18591317 - California poppies
Pexels - 414414-640-Cosmos
Pexels - 18860041- Mesquite tree
Pixabay 6170-1024-10242 - Desert willow
Pexels - 22350-640 - Date palm
Adobe - 61y-1 SVEGnlL_AC_SX679-Rosemary plant
Pexels - 4096492 - Purple cornflower
Adobe - 85c5d271-54-54ddbcdd5d3416 - Sedum
Pexels - 18784378 - Sunflower
Pexels - 883096-1280 Bee hotel
Pexels - 247165783 - rock steps and wall
Pixabay – 1595-584_1280 – Lavender
Pexels – lyn-ryan-18058892 – Hummingbird

References

New Mexico's Enchanted Xeriscape Guide https://www.ose.nm.gov/WUC/LearningXeriscape/XeriscapeGuide_ScreenResolution.pdf

Drought Stress Impacts on Plants and Different ... https://www.ncbi.nlm.nih.gov/pmc/articles/PMC7911879/

Top Ten Native Plants in the Desert Garden https://www.cactustocloud.org/native-garden

Water Conservation in Arid and Semi-Arid Regions https://www.eolss.net/sample-chapters/c07/E2-16-02-02.pdf

Principles Of Xeriscaping And Its Benefits - CYC Landscaping https://cyclandscaping.com/principles-of-xeriscaping-and-its-benefits/#:

Top 20 Drought-Tolerant Plants for a Waterwise Landscape https://www.gardendesign.com/plants/drought-tolerant.html

Landscaping With Crushed Rock & Gravel https://www.southwestboulder.com/blog/landscaping-with-crushed-rock-and-gravel

Mulching as water-saving technique in dryland agriculture https://bnrc.springeropen.com/articles/10.1186/s42269-019-0186-7

25 Desert Plants for a Vibrant Landscape https://www.gardendesign.com/desert/plants.html

10 Ways to Conserve Water in the Garden https://www.finegardening.com/project-guides/gardening-basics/10-ways-to-conserve-water-in-the-garden

Landscape Design with Native Plants https://extension.arizona.edu/sites/extension.arizona.edu/files/attachment/Landscape-Design-with-Native-Plants_2-2-2022_OLLI_for-MGA.pdf

Drought Tolerant Plants for a Florida-Friendly Landscape https://blogs.ifas.ufl.edu/orangeco/2020/03/11/drought-tolerant-plants-for-a-florida-friendly-landscape-zone-9/

Irrigation tips for desert gardens https://tucson.com/lifestyles/irrigation-tips-for-desert-gardens/article_c8ef8002-acf8-11eb-aca0-2b544da8b1a4.html

Safe Use of Household Greywater | New Mexico State University https://pubs.nmsu.edu/_m/M106/

Rainwater Harvesting 101 | Your How-To Collect ... https://www.watercache.com/education/rainwater-harvesting-101

Amending Soils for Water Conservation https://droughtresources.unl.edu/amending-soils-for-water-conservation

Mulching as a Sustainable Water and Soil Saving Practice ... https://www.mdpi.com/2073-4395/12/8/1881

Natural Garden Pest Control https://learn.eartheasy.com/guides/natural-garden-pest-control/

Article - Moisture Management: The Key to Composting https://www.cvcompost.com/moisture-management

Greening the Desert Project: Environmental Transformation https://www.goodstartpackaging.com/blog/greening-the-desert-project-environmental-transformation/

Water-Wise Wildlife Gardens: Drought-Tolerant Native Plants https://gardenforwildlife.com/blogs/learning-center/water-wise-wildlife-gardens-what-are-drought-tolerant-native-plants

Pollinator Conservation - Arizona-Sonora Desert Museum https://www.desertmuseum.org/center/pollinator_projects.php

Dry Climate Garden | 5 Ways to Save Water https://www.azplantlady.com/2022/05/5-ways-to-save-water-in-the-dry-climate-garden.html

Pollinator-Friendly Native Plant Lists https://xerces.org/pollinator-conservation/pollinator-friendly-plant-lists

25 Desert Plants for a Vibrant Landscape https://www.gardendesign.com/desert/plants.html

How to Improve and Manage Soils of Arid Climates http://www.agroconection.com/soil/how-to-improve-and-manage-soils-of-arid-climates/#:

Windbreak Benefits and Design - USU Extension https://extension.usu.edu/smallfarms/files/WindbreakBenefitsAndDesign.pdf

5 Steps for Erosion Control on Steep Slopes and Embankments https://www.denbow.

com/5-erosion-control-steps-steep-slopes-embankments/

Exploring the Latest Trends in Smart Irrigation Technology https://optconnect.com/trends-in-smart-irrigation-technology/

Innovative Solutions for Drought: Evaluating Hydrogel ... https://www.mdpi.com/2073-4441/15/11/1972

Drought-tolerant hybrid seed offers farmers reprieve from ... https://www.cimmyt.org/news/drought-tolerant-hybrid-seed-offers-farmers-reprieve-from-hunger/

Urban Water Conservation Policies in the United States https://agupubs.onlinelibrary.wiley.com/doi/full/10.1029/2017EF000797

www.ingramcontent.com/pod-product-compliance
Lightning Source LLC
Chambersburg PA
CBHW040933030426
42337CB00001B/4